THIRD EDITION

A Better High

Laugh, help, run, love...
and other ways to get
naturally high!

Matt Bellace, Ph.D.

Inspired by the nationally renowned youth program
"How to Get High Naturally"

A Better High

Matt Bellace, Ph.D.

T H I R D   E D I T I O N

ISBN: 978-1-936214-56-3
Library of Congress Control Number: 2011940737

Edited by Lisa Pliscou.
Proofread by Karen Kibler.

Attention Schools & Businesses:
This book is available at quantity discounts with bulk purchase for educational,
business, or sales promotional use. For information, please contact
Matt Bellace, Ph.D. Presentations, LLC at matt@mattbellace.com

Wyatt-MacKenzie Publishing
DEADWOOD, OREGON

Wyatt-MacKenzie Publishing, Inc, Deadwood, Oregon
www.WyattMacKenzie.com

For Roy and Sidney

Contents

Introduction

You may have a different experience reading this book if you haven't seen my presentation. If that's the case, don't feel bad—there are people in my *family* who don't entirely get what I do because they've never seen my program. If you *have* seen my program, then you already know how I talk about a difficult topic (substance abuse) to a difficult audience (teens) via stand-up comedy. You also know that I can make my point with passion and without getting preachy.

I think adults can get preachy when speaking to young people because they're projecting their own fear onto them. It makes sense, too. By the time you make it to adulthood, you've seen or lived through a fair number of hairy experiences and it scares you to think it could happen to "kids nowadays." You think that if you can just get young people to understand how scared you are for them, they might change their behavior. If it was only that easy!

I'll admit, I can have preachy tendencies, too. At the ripe old age of 40, I've seen my fair share of what we grownups like to call "cautionary tales." In fact, I'm going to get it out of my system right now. Here, in this introduction, I'm going to do my best impression of an adult preaching on this topic to you. By doing this, I hope you'll see that I've got those adult thoughts and feelings. The truth is, I'm afraid for young people. As a parent, I'm especially afraid for my kids. However, I hope that after you finish the introduction, and then the rest of the book, you'll also see that using humor can be a powerfully effective way to deliver this message.

Ready? Here I go.

We live in a society that all too often sends out the message that we need drugs in order to cope with life. The message is that if you're sad, you need a pill. If you're stressed, you need a drink. If you're psychotic . . . well, you may actually need something then.

We're force-fed advertisements trying to convince us that we can't "run" without Dunkin', sleep without Ambien, or hit the beach without a Corona. Pop culture floods us with images of young people binge-drinking and using drugs without consequences. It's evident in the happy endings of every *Hangover* movie or the playful tone of soon-to-be forgotten songs like *Wasted* by Tiesto or *Stay High* by Tove Lo. It's as if people have unthinkingly accepted the idea that there's a new stage of human development called "the wasted years." I can almost hear The Who song "Baba O'Riley"—better known as "Teenage Wasteland"—playing in my ear, with Roger Daltrey crying out at the end: "They're all wasted!" Well, I don't think they have to be. It doesn't *have* to be this way.

The hard-core truth is that lots of companies, and lots of people, are making tons of money by keeping people—often young people—using, abusing, and getting addicted to various substances. Drug companies profit from selling more prescriptions than anyone needs; medical marijuana dispensaries profit from selling pot to people without serious illnesses; street-level drug dealers profit from selling to kids. Big Tobacco, hurting from an historic drop in cigarette sales, have now turned to selling vapor pens that burn liquid nicotine. No one really knows yet what vaping does to you, but Big Tobacco pushes forward like those lawsuits of the 1980s never happened. Let's not forget companies that make powdered caffeine to sprinkle on your cereal or offer delivery services bringing weed and cocaine by bike. (I hear the coke guy is faster.)

"Big Food" companies, and even the government itself, are no better. State governments profit from exploiting gambling, alcohol, and marijuana addicts, even though in reality it costs much more to pay for rehab, healthcare, and prison terms when these behaviors get out of hand. Food companies profit from selling processed junk injected with chemicals, sugar, salt, and fat—all things which trigger the brain to keep consuming. In the typical supermarket there are aisles and aisles of what might seem like a tempting array of different foods, but so much of it contains high-fructose corn syrup that you'd think it was a vitamin. (It's not, and there's an increasing amount of evidence showing just how it contributes to America's worsening weight problem.) In the end, with all this money being taken out of everybody's wallets and pockets, it's you, your family, your town, and your local hospital that have to deal with the consequences.

All this has added up to a kind of complacency about drugs and drug use and young people can't help but see it. Over and over I hear students debate about which drug is worse—"Alcohol or marijuana?"—as if you should be choosing one over the other. It reminds me of my time working in a psychiatric hospital and hearing patients debating with each other about who was more mentally ill. And I'm thinking, "Does it matter? You're all in a psych ward!" Bottom line is, alcohol and marijuana are *both* drugs and they both have different side effects and neither one helps the developing brain. If you're under the age of 25, it may surprise you to learn that your brain is still actively changing and developing, making all kinds of neural connections that you'll use for the rest of your life. It may also surprise you to learn that behaviors like using alcohol and other drugs can change and sometimes damage those connections, and can influence your behavior. Personally, I wouldn't want a *substance* to be in control of my behavior. I prefer making terrible decisions all on my own!

I don't accept the message that we need a drug, or drugs, to cope with everyday life. I don't accept the notion that we need drugs so that we can enjoy a party. I do believe we *can* handle the ups and downs of life, even though it can sometimes be difficult. I believe we *can* feel genuine happiness without the aid of a pill. And you know what? It's courageous to face life without needing a drink. It's empowering to deal with emotional pain using your own strength, your own coping techniques. It's freeing to know that you don't have to buy food or drinks that are laden with chemicals. You can live a better life than what's portrayed in the media. You can live naturally high!

Chapter 1

How to Get High Naturally

A woman said to me, "You don't drink?
What a great accomplishment!"
"Thanks," I answered. "I also have a Ph.D."
She paused, then said, "Yeah, but not drinking...
How do you do it?"
—Matt Bellace

Good Pain vs. Bad Pain

The reconstructive knee surgery I had in 2007 taught me the difference between good pain and bad pain. When I woke up in the recovery room, my leg was in a machine that was bending it every 30 seconds. I was fine until the anesthesia wore off and I started making noises only dogs and mice could hear.

My surgeon, Dr. Russell Warren, is the team doctor for the New York Giants and a man of few words. He watched me struggle on the machine and said, "You have to do this for the next six weeks, six hours a day, every day." I was devastated. Then he said, "But this is the good pain." I was thinking, "If that's the good pain, what's the bad pain? Punching me repeatedly in the groin?"

Dr. Warren continued, "If you don't do this your knee will scar over and you might have a limp for the rest of your life." Then he looked at me and said, "But it's up to you," and left the room. I was thinking, "It's up to me? Pull the plug!"

For eight long weeks, when I wasn't at home on that machine, I was on non–weight-bearing crutches. That experience taught me that snow and ice are not your friend. Also not your friend: tornados. I met a student in Kansas who survived a tornado while on crutches. I asked him, "Did people help you?" He said, "No. They just yelled, 'Get down!'" I also learned that people love to guess what happened to you. I often heard "Was it skiing?" That is so rude, especially if I don't even know you. Would you go up to a stroke patient in a wheelchair and ask, "Was it smoking?" No, that would be terrible.

I am not ashamed to admit that there were moments during that time when I cried because it hurt so badly. But every time I wanted to pull the plug and quit, I realized that if I did I would be a hypocrite. How could I talk to students about good pain and then give up when facing it myself?

Young people have it tough because they're faced with so many examples of pain when they're young. It hurts to turn off a favorite television show and study for an exam, doesn't it? It can hurt to stand up and be a leader at your school. It hurts to tell someone at a party, "I don't want to drink." I guarantee no young person will ever turn down a beer and then skip away singing a song. This is not the movie *Frozen*. You'll never hear "No thanks for the beer! Let it go! Let it go!"

Good pain is good because you'll rarely regret it. I don't know any successful adult who says, "Can you believe I have all these degrees and awards? They're all over my large home. I'm so ashamed."

The bad pain is reserved for people who choose to take the easy way out. They'd rather cheat on a test than put in the work. They'd rather complain about life than actually stand up and make a difference. They'd rather have trust issues with their parents than tell their friends no. These examples qualify as bad pain because the negative consequences that can come from them aren't easily fixed.

Failing out of college, an inability to be a leader in your life, and trust issues with parents are complicated to resolve. They cost you time, money, and energy going backwards to try and make things right. It's much better to choose the good pain now over the bad pain later. It will still be painful, but the time, money, and energy you expend will push you forward. But—to quote my pal Dr. Warren—"It's up to you."

Positive Prevention

I've been fortunate for over a decade to travel the country and speak with young people about making healthy choices. As you might expect, adolescents are usually thrilled when they hear there'll be another assembly related to not doing drugs. The e-mails I receive from students after my programs often begin with "When I heard there was going to be a drug speaker, I thought, 'This is going to suck. I'll just sleep through it.'"

There was an assembly at a New Jersey high school that I'll never forget. During my opening interactive exercise, which involves several student volunteers on stage, a student grabbed the microphone from me and asked, "Are you one of those B.S. speakers who's going to tell us not to drink or do drugs when you've never drank or done drugs?" I was shocked. A student had never grabbed my microphone before, let alone asked a question that made me think, "All right then! Goodbye, everybody!"

I paused for a second and then delivered an answer that I still share with others to this day. I said, "I'm here today to talk to you about enjoying your life without using alcohol and other drugs. If you really want to understand that lifestyle and what it's like to grow up that way, than you need to hear from someone who's lived it. I've lived it. I've traveled the country for over fifteen years speaking about it and I'd like to share what I've learned with you."

I could tell instantly that my response helped the audience connect with me. I could sense that they were more accepting of my message. It's rare for an audience member to be so abrupt with me, but it's great to know that the message can withstand such scrutiny.

I was lucky to have learned from watching some great speakers and legendary comedians how to entertain while making a point. More importantly, I never say "Don't do drugs" because I know that won't stop young people from doing drugs. It will, however, stop them from listening to me. Instead I share laughs, some of my story, and insights from patients who I've treated. In the end, if students walk away from my program having heard me out, then I win and so do they. Honestly, it's a victory that after so many years I don't live in a van down by the river.

Telling people how to live their life doesn't change behavior. If it did, psychotherapy would last one session and everyone would be cured. Real behavioral change takes empathy, guidance, and time. I usually only get an hour or so to have an impact on an audience, so I choose to focus on supporting positive choices.

Psychologists believe it's easier to shape behavior by supporting a positive choice rather than punishing a negative one. The first major goal of my program is to use humor to connect with the audience. If they associate laughter with my message of natural highs, I've been partly successful. A second major goal is to integrate into the flow of the program user-friendly information about how the brain produces highs. When I've heard comments like "We didn't even realize we were learning until it was over," I know that goal was achieved. Finally, my third goal is to empower audience members to consider making changes in their life—especially in their decisions about alcohol and drugs. If successful, my program either validates their decisions to not use (if they don't drink or do drugs) or models a healthier lifestyle than they are living and encourages them seek change.

To accomplish my program goals, I structure the talk by presenting an acronym—L.E.A.D. I created the acronym because it helps the audience remember what I talked about, but I also believe that living a naturally high lifestyle requires being a leader in your own life.

The four points of L.E.A.D. are:
· Leaning on healthy people for support
· Expressing your emotions in a healthy way
· Achieving natural highs every day, and
· Don't be afraid to take a stand.

Lean on Healthy People for Support

I went to Montclair High School in Montclair, New Jersey. It was a school known for having great football teams. I played football at MHS, which still surprises me since I'm built more like a reader. During my junior year, I was the backup quarterback and we were ranked #1 in the state and #6 in the *USA Today* Top 25 poll.

The 1990 season was the most memorable in the school's history. Cue Bruce Springsteen's "Glory Days"!

We lost the state championship that season in what the New Jersey *Star-Ledger* later dubbed "The Greatest Game of the Century." The loss occurred on our home field in front of 13,000 fans, who thought they had witnessed Montclair winning a state title. However, a controversial call gave our opponent, Randolph High School, a chance to kick the winning field goal as time expired. That season was quite memorable for Randolph, too. Their head coach had passed away during the season and his son took over the team and kept a state record winning streak alive. We later learned that the team visited the deceased coach's grave the night before the champion game. The story is so legendary in New Jersey that I'm surprised there isn't a movie about it. There might be, but I just can't watch another high school football movie.

A few years back, Randolph High School invited me to present my natural highs program to the entire school. They had no knowledge of my football history, so I was fine with it aside from the fact that they had ruined my life. During my presentation, I said, "The game ended with a controversial call," which got a huge laugh for some reason. Then I told them I had been on the losing team and they cheered. I replied, "Yeah, well, I heard you haven't won much since." To their credit, they laughed and it really *was* funny because they hadn't won in a long time. A few months later they beat Montclair again in the state championship. I still speak at Randolph, but I'm done making jokes about their football team.

I feel like being part of that game was a blessing in disguise. It taught me that life goes on after a big loss. It wasn't the first time in my life that I'd dealt with loss, pain, or failure. At a young age, I experienced rejection, got poor grades, and even lost family members to illness and death. Every decade of my life had some element of loss, pain, and feelings of failure. However, I learned that the key ingredient to getting through the experience is about having friends and family to lean on. I remember hugging my mom after the game and then crying. It seems silly now to cry over something like that, but it was really important then to know that someone was there for me. My friends were also there; I could talk and laugh about it with them, which felt therapeutic.

I wasn't going on to a career in football, so learning about the importance of leaning on people for support may have been more helpful to me than winning that game. In retrospect, I wish every player on our team had taken something positive from that experience.

The next year, I started at quarterback and we opened the season against our archrival Bloomfield High School. One of our star players from last year's powerhouse team showed up to cheer us on. He had graduated, but got arrested over the summer for selling drugs, and was out on parole. The guy was such an amazing athlete. The season before, I'd have given anything to trade places with him. That night, he looked like a guy without a friend. I wonder if he wanted to be me that night. I don't know if he had people to lean on after losing the state championship, but I have to believe that a lack of positive influences contributed to his poor outcome.

Leaning on healthy people for support could be the most important part of living a naturally high lifestyle. If you're surrounded by positive support, it can encourage you to step outside of your comfort zone and try new things. This is why the National Institute of Drug Abuse lists the number-one protector against adolescent substance abuse as strong and positive social support.

This support can be in the form of friends, family, religious or service organizations, teachers, and/or coaches. It's not who or what it is, but the quality of the support that matters. In my opinion, it's especially important to have a small group of fun, supportive friends you can rely upon. Let's face it—the right friends can even make waiting in line fun.

If you feel like your support is made up of some negative influences, I can sympathize. I grew up in an Italian family in northern New Jersey with a dad who looked like a smaller version of Tony Soprano. In some ways my family acted like the Sopranos, too. No one ever got decapitated, but I heard plenty of critical comments and negativity. When the stock market collapsed in the fall of 2008, someone asked me if my father—who worked on Wall Street for over 30 years—was upset. I said, "Upset? He's the most relaxed I've ever seen him. He's been waiting for this his entire life."

I am fortunate that despite any negativity in my family, they also happen to be supportive. They've always been there for me when it mattered most. I am also fortunate that they're healthy and that I get to spend time with them. However, telling jokes about my family is how I cope with their eccentricities.

I developed this coping mechanism at an early age. The most difficult period for my family during my lifetime occurred while I was in middle school. I watched arguments on an almost nightly basis between my brother and my parents. These arguments were centered on my brother and his poor adolescent choices. My brother is five years older than me and in high school he was very social. He hung out with the party-holic crowd. They were into drinking, drugs, and other high-risk behaviors. The fact that many young people his age were doing it was really not an excuse. What seemed to upset my parents most was that my brother would get caught doing something wrong and then defend his behavior rather than take responsibility for it. He would yell at them and say, "You're just jealous!" In my head I thought, "Jealous of what? You have no money and no car."

The way I coped with all the arguments was to find humor in the pain. Fortunately for me there were a lot of funny moments. Like the day my brother decided he was going to be blond. So he got this spray called Sun-In—similar to bleach—poured it all over his black hair, and went out into the sun. Two hours later his head looked like an orange highlighter. That happened to be the week my father decided to take the family picture. To this day, in my parents' living room there is a big picture of three Bellaces and Danny Bonaduce.

When all the yelling first broke out, I'd go to my room. Eventually, I became so used to it that I stayed for all the great material. One time my brother was being lectured on why beer was bad for teenagers and he responded, "Relax, I heard there's protein in beer."

My brother failed out of college after his first semester. To be fair, he technically could have returned, but my parents felt that he wasn't even trying. I find it ironic that all the partying and rebelling against my parents landed him in the one place you'd think he'd be horrified to end up—back home. Coincidentally, seven years ago his former college invited me to speak to their freshmen at orientation. They had no idea about the connection. I'm happy to say that they invited me back and at this point, I think I've spent more time on their campus than my brother did.

As I look back, two positive things came out of my brother's turmoil. First, the bad pain of failing out of college and having to pay my parents back for his first semester's tuition likely helped him focus, take responsibility, and get his life back on track. My brother made a big change when he started at a new school. He surrounded himself with more supportive people—including fraternity brothers and learning specialists—to help him get through.

I'm very proud of him for putting his life back together and moving in a positive direction. There are so many examples of people who just give up after failing out of college, never to return. He never gave up and that is honorable.

I talk about my brother in my programs, and afterwards, one of the most frequent questions I get is "How's your brother doing now?" He's doing well and we are closer than ever. In fact, he's married to a wonderful woman now and they have a beautiful son, my nephew Mateo! I think my brother is in a much better place today than he was years ago. To be honest, I never thought I would see him get married. He used to be so afraid of commitment that if I met a girl he was dating he'd tell me, "She's not the one, dude." I was thinking, "That's OK, but she's still in the car."

The second best thing to come out of those days was my decision, when I was in eighth grade, not to drink or do drugs. (We live in such a crazy time, who could imagine that making a decision like I did would be the basis for a speaking career.) One night I announced at the dinner table, "I will never drink or do drugs."

I imagined my mom would be so happy she would just hug me and say, "Son, you have no curfew. You can drive the car." I'd be like, "Mom, I'm only twelve." She would say, "It doesn't matter."

For some reason, my announcement didn't impress her as much as I thought it would. I guess all those years dealing with my brother's behavior made her too wary. Two years later, in the summer of 1989, when I was a sophomore at Montclair High, my mother sent me to a leadership and prevention conference called the Teen Institute of the Garden State (T.I.G.S.). I guess she didn't send me as much as she *made* me go.

It was the last week of summer vacation and I was so mad at

her that I started making up lies to get out of it. I said, "Mom, I heard this conference is just for recovering alcoholics." My mom hated that one. When I arrived at the camp there were counselors on stage, in crazy costumes, cheering loudly, and I said, "Look! They're still drinking!"

It didn't matter to my mom, because she would have never let me leave. She was the vice principal at my high school and a tough woman. Guys would stop me in the hall and say, "I'm going to kill you. Your mom gave me two weeks' detention." To which I would reply, "I'm not afraid of you. I live with her."

T.I.G.S. was a statewide prevention program which empowered students to be drug-free. The camp was deep in the woods outside of Blairstown, New Jersey. Yes, New Jersey has deep woods. It featured ropes courses, great motivational speakers/comedians, and small group discussions. I can still remember how great it felt to have an adult ask me for my opinion and actually listen nonjudgmentally. The best part was making friends from other schools and of course, the four-to-one girl-to-guy ratio.

As I look back on it now, the conference did something very progressive. They didn't use scare tactics to convince young people to behave. Scare tactics have been proven not to work when it comes to drug and alcohol prevention. In fact, I had a speaker come to my middle school once and yell at us, "If you do drugs, you're gonna die!" I thought, "Why are you yelling?" Then I went out to a bunch of parties, saw classmates of mine drinking and doing drugs, and I would think, "Nobody's dead. That speaker's wrong!"

Every year in this country, alcohol and drugs kill over 100,000 people. And celebrities, with all their wealth and power, are not exempt from this grim statistic. Some recent casualties are Robin Williams, Amy Winehouse, Cory Monteith, Philip Seymour Hoffman, Justin Bieber's career. If you take a close look at the lives and deaths of some celebrities, you'll notice that it often takes a decade or more for drugs to kill them. The reason scare tactics don't work is that alcohol and drug abuse doesn't kill you fast enough. That's a pretty dark thing to say, but what do you think would happen if one teen died every time there was a drinking or drug party in your town? Well, first of all people would walk real slowly into those parties. They'd be saying,

"Who's it going to be tonight? Not it!"

If drug and alcohol abuse killed one student at every party, the problem with drugs and alcohol would practically disappear in this country. Psychology teaches us that punishing something quickly and consistently can change behavior. The problem with drug and alcohol abuse is that it can go on for years before the user feels the bad pain from his or her negative behaviors.

The folks at the T.I.G.S. conference somehow knew that scare tactics don't work. Instead, they focused on empowerment. They inspired us to try and achieve greatness in our lives. I'm not sure everyone responded, but I did. I got the message: if you want to be better than you are today, you have to *want* to be healthy. I was all about internal motivation to do something positive. By the time the five days ended, I went from hating it to loving it. I went from dying to leave to dying to come back as one of those crazy costumed counselors.

I was rejected the first time I tried to return to T.I.G.S as a counselor. I can laugh about it now, but back then it was devastating. The following year I matured quite a bit and reapplied. This time I was accepted and went on to have a great experience. In fact, it was during that counselor year that I bonded with all of those supportive friends that I still hold so dear. The responsibilities of the counselors at camp included putting on skits, role-modeling healthy behavior, and genuinely helping others. If you were really lucky, you'd be asked to speak in front of the camp.

Dave Johnston, the leader of the counselors, saw something in me and made sure that I would speak to the group. It was probably less than five minutes, but the experience gave me my first taste of being a social activist. The camp environment was supportive of self-expression and provided a nonjudgmental atmosphere to try something new like public speaking. Yet, without the support of the friends I met there, I would have had little chance to continue this positive behavior back home.

Try This: Are you interested in attending a Teen Institute or high school prevention conference like it? There are almost a dozen active programs in the U.S. under the umbrella of the National Association of Teen Institutes (www.teeninstitute.org). Today, New Jersey's Teen Institute is called the Lindsey Meyer

Teen Institute (www.lmteeninstitute.org), named after an inspirational young woman who attended the program in the late 1990s.

There are also very similar, popular programs around the country—such as Youth to Youth International (www.y2yint.com) and Students Against Destructive Decisions (www.sadd.org)—that also have great local and national conferences that do much the same as the one I attended in 1989.

Pick Your Brain:
Environment

Reading science articles doesn't cause me to break out a highlighter much these days. I guess after 21 years of school I've done enough of that. However, the June 25, 2006 edition of the *New York Times* had me highlighting like an eighth grader again. In a great article called "An Anti-Addiction Pill," by Benoit Denizet-Lewis, there was a reference to a study called "Rat Park."[1]

This was an elegant 1980s research study performed by Dr. Bruce Alexander from the Department of Psychology at Simon Fraser University in British Columbia, Canada.[2] The hypothesis was simple: rats that lead stressful, boring lives would self-medicate (in this case, drink a sweet substance with a heroin-like drug in it) when given the chance, and rats with stimulating, lower-stress lives would not self-medicate.

Dr. Alexander first constructed two very different rat environments. The low-stress environment was called "Rat Park" and it provided ample access to food and water, along with natural vegetation and rat toys. You know—rat iPods, rat Xboxes, etc. The high-stress environment was much smaller, more isolating, and had no toys. The one similarity among the two environments was access to a sweet drink containing a heroin-like substance that the rats could drink when desired—rats love sweet drinks.

After a week, they measured the amount of heroin-like drink consumed by the rats living in the two environments. The results were surprising. The "Rat Park" animals were having too much fun to drink more than a little of the heroin drink, regardless of how sweet Dr. Alexander made it. The isolated and stressed rats, on the other hand, often got high, drinking more than a dozen times the amount of the heroin drink as the "Rat-Parkers." Other studies since have supported the notion that environment can play a big role in the behavior of drug abuse.[3,4]

There have been numerous studies over the past three decades that make the case for the role of genetics in addictive behaviors. However, the Alexander study serves as an important reminder that the interaction between a person's genes and their environment can have a significant influence over their behavior. A stimulating and supportive environment—especially during childhood and adolescence—is a strong protector against addiction. Addicts are more likely to have been stressed during childhood and they are less able to deal with stress as adults.[4] These stresses can include neglect; emotional, physical, or sexual abuse; and poverty.

Studies show that animals stressed during early development are more likely to self-administer drugs later in life.[3] In contrast, living in an enriched, lower-stress environment appears to protect animals from developing addictive behaviors.[1] If we assume that humans react to stress in similar ways, then this process is being played out in families all across the country.

Express Your Emotions in a Healthy Way

My wife and I are both psychologists, which means
we have very short arguments.
"Do you know how that makes me feel, Matt?"
"Yes, I do. I'm afraid that's all the time we have left."
—Matt Bellace

In my presentations, I ask students to raise their hand if they think their parents are good listeners. What kind of response do you think I get? Five hands, maybe ten? You may be surprised to hear that usually 25% or more of the students raise their hands. At national leadership conferences with some of the brightest student leaders, I've seen 95% or more. And I find that the more hands go up for that question, the more attentive the audience is in listening to me. I've never seen any research on it, but I suspect that young people with good listeners at home are able to model that behavior at school. It may also inspire them to be better students and get more involved in leadership positions.

When I was growing up, I felt like my parents were terrible listeners. If my dad got bored with the conversation, he would just get up and leave. That hurts when you were the only two people in the room. And my mom had a habit of interrupting after three seconds and saying, "This is what you should do." It didn't matter what the topic was. For example, one time I started to tell her about a test not going well and she immediately said, "This is what you should do. Go back tomorrow and tell them to give you the test again." I held back from letting her know it was the SAT's. They're not giving it again tomorrow.

The problem is if you don't have anyone at home who listens to you well, especially during adolescence, it can lead to feeling emotionally disconnected. I was lucky that my mom sent me to the L.M.T.I. camp where I met both kids my age *and* adults who were amazing listeners and were so supportive. That experience really changed my life. Thanks, Mom, for making me go!

Many young people tell me that they are under a lot of pressure to "be perfect." I understand that to mean they feel they need to achieve straight A's in the highest-level classes, make the varsity team, and be popular. If they should fall short of these expectations, some believe they won't get into the best college, get the best job, or have the best life. (Whatever "best" might mean.) So where does all this pressure come from? It comes from our society and our media, which put perfect-looking people on pedestals, as if demanding that we admire and try to emulate them. The pressure can also come from parents, some of whom will threaten school districts with lawsuits if their son or daughter experiences a little failure or what they think is unfair treatment. You know what? Unfair things happen to students—and everybody else—all the time. However, learning how to live through it is going to serve young people better than simply having their parents make it go away, like they're waving a magic wand.

Grandparents can sometimes be the better listeners in a family. They've got more life experience, a little objectivity, and quite possibly more free time, so they can often remove excessive emotion from their half of the conversation. I remember my grandparents being so warm and unconditionally loving, espe-

cially my grandfather. He was one of those larger-than-life characters who made everyone he met feel special. He was the mayor
of his town, a small-business owner, and, in my family, an icon.

My grandfather passed away when I was going into eighth
grade. He died of cancer and it was horrible to watch, though I
never once heard him complain. I remember feeling incredibly
helpless those final months. I remember after one particularly
difficult visit with him in the hospital, my brother and I went out
fishing on the local dock. My grandfather used to take us to that
dock when we were younger and we had a great time whether
we caught fish or not. That trip without him was the last one. It
just didn't feel right.

In the months after his passing, my brother went to college
and started partying like it was his major. Knowing what I know
now, I would say he was "self-medicating the pain with alcohol
and other drugs." Back then, I was angry at him and didn't understand the need for all the drama. I clearly remember thinking,
"There's no way *I'm* making the same mistakes. I'm going to do
something important with my life!" There weren't any eighth-
graders at my school curing cancer, so sports became my way to
express my emotions. In high school, I was co-captain of both the
baseball and wrestling teams, and quarterback on the football
team, but I wasn't a gifted athlete. I just worked hard. Sports
served as a wonderful outlet to help me cope with my emotional
pain.

It turns out I'm not the only one who turned to sports to
cope. Recently, I spoke at a high school in Richmond, Virginia. In
the front row was a young lady named Anna Wilson, who bravely
volunteered for one of my demonstrations during the presentation. Anna told me that her brother is Seattle Seahawks
quarterback Russell Wilson. If you don't happen to know this
already, he led the Seahawks to a Super Bowl victory in 2013. I
also learned during the trip that during Russell's time at this same
high school, his father became quite sick and would eventually
pass away in 2010. According to media interviews, Russell's dad
was incredibly supportive of him. Russell was quoted after the
Super Bowl as saying, "I remember my dad asking me one time,
and it's something that has always stuck with me: 'Why not you,
Russ?'" He was referring to Russell achieving his dreams in
athletics and it struck me as such an amazing and uncondition-

ally loving and supportive thing to say to your child. I can't imagine how tough it must have been to lose such a positive parental role model.

One of Russell's middle-school teachers, who now works at the high school and saw me speak, told me about her experiences with Russell during that difficult time. She said that it appeared the challenge of dealing with his dad's illness transformed him from a student with lots of athletic potential, but who was struggling behaviorally, into a superstar athlete and eventually a role model for the entire high school. Instead of becoming self-destructive, it propelled him to greater heights. He's not the only one either. As Malcolm Gladwell points out in his insightful book on how underdogs defeat the odds, *David and Goliath*, an unusually high number of famous actors, athletes, and politicians lost a parent at an early age. For them, pain and suffering were like fuel that inspired grand accomplishments.

The reason it's so important to express yourself in a healthy way has to do with coping skills. If you don't have healthy outlets for dealing with stress, then alcohol or other drugs can easily become your outlet. I was reminded of this during my predoctoral internship at Mount Sinai Medical Center in New York City. One of my rotations was on the traumatic brain injury unit. It was rewarding, but it was also the most difficult job I've ever had. One patient in particular taught me an unforgettable lesson about self-expression.

"E"—I don't want to use his real name—was dumped by his girlfriend one month before his high school graduation. He was angry and depressed. Like many high school students in that situation, he called up his friends, told them what happened, and they did the stereotypical thing—they took him out and got him drunk. E returned home around two in the morning, drunk and more emotional than before he left. Alcohol abuse intensifies emotions. If you're angry before you use, you can become really angry while intoxicated. If you're depressed before you use, you could even become suicidal once you do.

I don't know if E attempted suicide that night, but I do know that he got on a motorcycle—without a helmet—and managed to drive himself into a tree. He suffered a severe brain injury. When E awoke in the hospital, he couldn't move anything on the left side of his body. He couldn't talk clearly and he was so confused that he kept trying to pull the tubes out of his arms. The doctors had to put restraints on him. As I watched that young man struggle through the early phases of a head injury, I learned that there are far worse things in life than death.

It took E three months to begin to walk and communicate again. I met with E every day and my job was to assess his cognitive ability and talk to him about his emotions. One day, I asked him about the night of the accident. I asked him if he'd wanted to hurt himself. He looked at me and said, "I don't know what happened that night, but I can tell you that there's got to be a better way to deal with getting dumped." E will probably have cognitive and physical deficits for the rest of his life, but even he understood the downside of using alcohol to cope with intense emotions.

That's one example of a teen with poor coping skills who learned the hard way about the bad pain. A more common situation usually involves a poor choice that costs time and energy more than anything else.

In the spring of 2010, I was speaking at a school in Tacoma, Washington. One thousand high school students in a gym—not exactly an intimate environment. Halfway into my program it was going pretty well until a student in the back row tried to heckle me. Addressing a heckler is always challenging for me because in comedy we're trained to quickly annihilate the person, but making a student cry is not why I was hired.

I couldn't even see this particular student, but I made a few mild jokes about what a nightmare he must be in class if he couldn't sit through an hour of comedy. Then he stood up and started yelling at the top of his lungs, but he was so far away I couldn't hear him. I made a joke about how I was from New York so I wasn't scared by yelling and then a teacher escorted him out of the assembly. As they left, I said, "You seem so angry I think you're going to meet me in the parking lot."

And he did. I was rolling my duffle bag out of the school with two students escorting me. They were laughing and saying, "We're your bodyguards." Then they took one look at him coming across the parking lot and ran the other way! Now I'm standing out there with this lunatic and his two goons who want to punch me in the face. His name, by the way, was Casanova. Honestly, I find that pretty hilarious because if your parents name you

Casanova, you've got two choices in life—you're a lover or you kill people. He wanted to kill me, so he got into a boxing position and raised his fists.

I looked him in the eye and after all my years of psychology training said, "Violence is not the answer." He should have punched me just for saying that. Of course, in the back of my mind I was hoping security would show up and taze him. Luckily the vice-principal showed up and we all left.

I was later told that because of his behavior Casanova was expelled from school, which I thought was appropriate, but still such a waste of time and energy. The real reason he was expelled was because he didn't know how to cope with negative emotions without resorting to violent behavior. This little scenario played out for me in a very public way, but it's scary to imagine what students in school or online face when dealing with classmates who have little self-control.

Anyway, if all that drama wasn't crazy enough, the next morning I was speaking at a school in the area and the whole time I was paranoid that Casanova would show up and shank me. The presentation went well and the coast was clear on the way to my car. As I put the key in the ignition, I heard a loud knock at my window. I jumped about a mile and spun my head around. A student was giving me the thumbs-up sign and saying, "Good job, dude!" I think I peed myself right there.

One of my favorite books is M. Scott Peck's *The Road Less Traveled*. Peck was a psychiatrist who wrote about a common problem among many of his patients—they believed that life *should* be easy. The problem with this thinking is life is often not easy. Peck noticed that when his patients would encounter a problem, they would rather complain about it or abuse themselves than face emotional pain. It was fascinating for me to hear about the great lengths some people would go to in order to avoid emotional pain. In many cases, their avoidance behaviors became part of their psychiatric conditions—like addictions to alcohol and other drugs.

Although Peck never used language like "natural highs," he did suggest finding healthier ways to express emotions. He supported having honest and caring conversations with someone who is a helpful, nonjudgmental listener. He encouraged people to be aware of emotions—good or bad—and not be afraid of them.

As I look back, my emotional outlets included sports in high school, listening to stand-up comedy, academics, and social activism in college. Today there are about a dozen ways in which I cope with stress and powerful emotions—without turning to harmful substances or hurting myself in other ways.

Running, cooking, and listening to great music are some of my favorites today. You may choose music, acting, or hanging out with friends. These are just a few possibilities. No matter what you choose, it should be an activity that tends to leave you feeling better when you're done.

Try This: Go to a quiet room, sit down, put your hand on your belly, and close your eyes. As you're sitting there, focus all of your mental energy on your breathing. (It's harder than you might think.) As you sit quietly, directing your mind to attend to nothing but breathing, you'll probably start noticing how many distractions there are around you. There may be outside noise or thoughts in your head. Don't force yourself to try and ignore these distractions. Instead, let them pass you by like they're floating down a river. Let them come and let them go and get back to thinking about breathing. Think about all aspects of your breathing, including the sensation of inhaling and exhaling, and the feeling of your belly going up and down. Do this for 30 seconds the first time and then, the next time, try for one minute. Keep trying this once a day until you reach fifteen minutes. It may be difficult at first, but there's mounting evidence that this simple activity will alter your nervous system in a way that'll help you cope more effectively with stress. Want some help getting started? Check out apps like Simply Being or Get Some Headspace.

Pick Your Brain:
Rewire Your Brain's Reaction to Stress

In recent years, using writing to express painful or traumatic experiences has become a favorite relaxation technique for many psychologists to use with their patients. The technique sounds simple: write out the painful event and describe in detail every aspect of the event. It may sound like a horrible activity, but in the company of the right therapist, it actually works. The act of going through the painful details helps separate the emotion from the event. This technique has been found to have advantages over traditional therapy, because it can be done anywhere with almost any age group—particularly with people who have trouble in one-on-one conversations.[5] A recent study of depression-vulnerable college students showed that expressive writing for 20 minutes three days in a row lowered symptoms of depression for six months after the assignment.[6]

Expressive writing is believed to work by allowing the writer to express thoughts that would otherwise be suppressed. The ability to write out one's innermost thoughts and feelings can help to free the mind of those thoughts for the remainder of the day.

Carrying around a lot of emotional baggage can really take a toll on your mental abilities. Consider the brain function called "working memory," which is a form of memory that temporarily stores and utilizes small bits of information about the world around you. If your working memory is occupied by stressful thoughts, it's prevented from being used for everyday problem-solving and retention of information.

I don't want to get bogged down here talking about how not to get bogged down in your mind. However, if you're constantly thinking about what you're going to say to someone who really upset you, you may have higher levels of stress and less tolerance for waiting in line at the grocery store. A recent study showed that stressful thoughts and feelings are easier to deal with after a person has had a chance to free up their working memory through expressive writing.[7]

So the next time you get upset, try writing about the event. Make sure you write out as many details as you feel are necessary. It doesn't matter if you write it out by hand or on the computer. I wouldn't post it to a social networking site anytime soon though, unless you're directly messaging a supportive friend. If it's too painful the first time, try it again a few days later. In the days and weeks after you've finished writing about the event, pay attention to whether or not you feel any better about it. If you find expressive writing is particularly helpful, you may wish to make it a more regular activity.

Exposure to stressful events in life can make you mentally

tougher, provided the stressful events don't last for too long and you have a chance to recover. An important study in the 1990s used medical records to measure how many stressful events a child can sustain before his or her overall life outcome is negatively affected. It's known as the ACE study, which stands for Adverse Childhood Events, and it collected data from over 17,000 patients, including information about physical abuse, sexual abuse, emotional neglect, household dysfunction, and more. The group the researchers studied was relatively well-educated and financially stable, but a quarter of the participants grew up in a family with an alcoholic or a drug user. In fact, two-thirds of all the participants had experienced at least one ACE, and around 10% of them had four or more. It turns out that each incidence of childhood trauma resulted in an increase in negative outcomes, ranging from addictive behavior to chronic disease. The study revealed that people with ACE scores of four or higher were two times as likely to smoke and seven times as likely to be an addict than those with an ACE score of zero or one.

The human brain was designed to deal well with short-term stress, like chasing down an animal to catch for dinner. However, long-term, continual stress can make us sick. It's like training to run sprints for a year and then someone says, "You're fast, so today we're going to run a marathon." You'd probably get off to a good start because running is not a problem for you. Two hours later, though, your body's inability to handle continuous running would cause you to break down.

The reality is that none of us can completely avoid stress. If you want to be more resilient, it helps to live through *some* loss, pain, and failure. I don't wish these things upon you, but when the stress arrives—and it will—categorize it as either good pain or bad pain. The key is using coping techniques, like the breathing exercise I described earlier. Start with five minutes a day, progressing to fifteen minutes a day, and it will have profound effects on how you react to stress.

One example when the breathing worked for me occurred when I was out to dinner with my wife and one- year-old daughter. During the meal, my daughter pooped up her diaper so bad, it shot out the back and all over her clothing. My wife looked at me and said, "This one's yours." I picked my daughter up and thought, "I'll take her to the car, that's a good move!" Not really. I got to the car, opened her diaper, and she decided to start wiggling. A dirty diaper was now dangerously close to ruining the resale value of my car. I reached for the wipes and after the third pull they were all gone. I gasped for air, like I'd just lost my iPhone.

Immediately, the tension started building in my chest. I could feel little beads of sweat on my forehead, so I started the breathing exercises and got to work. I cleaned up my daughter and threw out the diaper. I took off her outfit and threw *it* out. I put on a new diaper and that's when I realized I didn't have another outfit. I walked back into a crowded restaurant with a half-naked child. I got our table and my wife had a stressed look on her face. "Do we have to leave?" she asked, and I replied, "No, keep eating."

A few minutes later, she asked, "What happened to you? You're so calm." My wife knows me. She knows that normally I would lose it in this type of situation, because even though I'm a psychologist, I'm also Italian. Interrupting a meal for any reason turns me into my own little version of Tony Soprano. However, on that night, the breathing exercises that I had been using helped me stay calm and make more rational decisions. The most important decision I made was not to react emotionally to the situation because there was nothing I could do except make my best effort.

So for you, dealing with a kid's poopy diaper may not be a big problem in your life right now, but I'm guessing you have your own stressful events to deal with. I encourage you to incorporate the breathing exercises into your daily routine. Let's say you're lying in bed and can't fall asleep. Thoughts are racing through your head about an upcoming test or a text message you got from a friend. Every time you tell yourself to stop thinking and fall asleep, it seems to make things just get worse. Then you begin the breathing exercises, and within seconds you give yourself permission to let the distractions enter your mind, but float away. Before you know it, you're asleep. I've been there. It's worked for me and it will likely work for you.

Neuroscience research has shown that this breathing exercise, often referred to as mindfulness mediation practice, can help someone react with less emotional during decision-making tasks.[8] A study performed at the Human Neuroimaging Laboratory at Virginia Tech demonstrated that meditators with a decade of experience were better than non-meditators at keeping calm during a decision-making game. The game involved accepting offers of money, some resulting in big payouts and others not so much. When the meditators made decisions, their brains showed less activity in areas associated with emotion and more activity in areas associated with deep thinking. The authors also commented that in comparing the locations of brain activity, there were significant differences between the meditators and non-meditators, suggesting that meditation training can profoundly alter how the brain actually functions.

Highly technical brain research on the topic of mindfulness mediation could fill a hundred books of this size. But if this area interests you, I suggest you start with some layperson's psychology. *Psychology Today* and *Scientific American Mind* are interesting magazines, and you might also like websites such as Inward Bound (www.ibme.info) or Guided Mindfulness Meditation (www.mindfulnesscds.com). Maybe look for a local class you can take. And some courses are offered for free online, along with meditation apps you can download.

Achieve Natural Highs Every Day

I caught my brother with weed and I said, "That's not good for you!"
He said, "Weed is like salad." I responded, "You don't put dressing on it!
I'm the younger brother—why am I telling you?"
—Matt Bellace

There are many types of proven natural highs. Running long distances, for example, releases opiates in the brain and allows runners to experience a sense of euphoria. My wife loves running—even in the dead of winter. When she goes out in the cold I tell her, "If you get lost, I'm not coming to get you." She even runs when she has a cold because she claims it makes her feel better.

Personally, as an Italian-American guy living in New York City, one of my natural highs is eating. You're my kind of person if you're thinking, "Thank you, Doctor Obvious—that explains why every movie about Italian-Americans seems to involve eating in a New York City restaurant." You may not know that eating releases small amounts of the feel-good chemical dopamine into your brain, which elevates your mood. Eating great food must release a ton of dopamine in my brain because I ate a pizza recently—at DiFara's in Brooklyn—that was so delicious my head almost exploded.

This book explores natural highs, such as running and eating, in more detail, but it also focuses on laughing, loving, helping, and other ways to create your own natural high in everyday life.

One of my favorite natural highs happened when I was in college. It all started when a friend of mine said, "Matt, we should duct-tape someone to a wall."

"Uh . . . okay," I replied. "Where did you learn that?"

He said, "Spanish TV. Telemundo."

So the next morning we asked a friend if she would stand on a chair in the student center and let us duct-tape her to the wall.

"Uh . . . okay," she said.

Once our friend was firmly duct-taped to the wall, we pulled the chair out from underneath her and ran away. We hid around the corner and watched other students' reactions as they walked to class and saw a human being stuck to the wall. Some people freaked out, like they weren't sure if they had done drugs or not. Others picked up a stick and started poking at her. My favorite reaction was from a student who grew up in New York City. He walked by, looked, and kept going. He was totally not impressed, like he'd seen it every day of his life.

I've told this story at hundreds of schools and after I leave, students at dozens of them have decided to duct-tape the principal to the wall. (In all cases, the principal was willing.) One school did the duct-tape activity as a fundraiser. They charged a dollar a strip and raised over $2,000. I think their principal is still up there.

By the way, if you or your school is going to duct-tape someone to a wall, there are a few things to keep in mind. First, you cannot just take someone and just stick them on a wall. You must *ask* first. To make this a true challenge, limit yourself to one roll of duct tape. Next, you must make sure to do it on a brick or concrete wall. If you choose a wall with wallpaper, the paper will probably come off (not good). Also, do not stick the person on a tree or traffic sign, because if you do the person might suffocate and die. I'm not kidding here. It's fun to do this as a competition between groups. Some schools enjoy doing it as a competition between grades. By the way—it's a lot harder than you think to put someone on a wall with only one roll of duct tape.

It's important to note that the natural highs presented in this book—if done to excess—can all be abused. For example, over one-third of children in this country suffer from obesity and the rewarding aspects of eating may play a role in that epidemic. On the opposite end of the spectrum, there are people who eat too little and exercise too much, conditions known as anorexia and exercise bulimia, respectively. My wife is a clinical psychologist who treats eating disorders and she opened my eyes to how a love for food or exercise can quickly turn into an unhealthy obsession.

One key element to achieving healthy natural highs is to incorporate them into a life that's balanced. If any activity you enjoy interferes with your academic, social, or emotional functioning, then it's out of balance. It may feel amazing to fall in love and be in a new relationship, but the natural high of loving someone is not worth failing out of school for.

In college, my natural high was sports. I can remember being a freshman and telling people my major was baseball. It was my honest opinion at the time, but it was naïve. If my life were just baseball in college, I'd have missed out on discovering a passion for psychology, taking road trips, and cooking—all of which started during my undergraduate years.

Another important element in achieving healthy natural highs is avoiding internal negativity. This type of negativity can actually be a natural high blocker. I almost did it to myself on a recent camping trip to Jackson Hole, Wyoming—a place where you can have a natural high by just opening your eyes.

An old high school friend, Paul Brown –who is a real-life *Man vs. Wild* type guy—was kayaking with me across Jackson Lake to our campsite. A few hours into our paddle trip, I started angrily swatting every fly that got near my face. I must have looked ridiculous swinging at the air while trying to keep from tipping over. It would have served me right to fall into the water. I was ruining the experience. Paul asked me what was wrong and I told him, "I hate these flies! If I stop swatting they're going to lay eggs in my ears!" That idea came from an internet article I read about a guy who had flies lay eggs that hatched in his ear. Paul heard this and told me I needed to spend less time reading blogs and more time enjoying the real world.

As I continued to whine, I realized that I was stressing myself out. Eventually I made the decision to adapt to the environment and accept the fact that in order to experience this once-in-a-lifetime natural high, I would have to live with a little discomfort. I'm happy to report that I was able to calm down and enjoy one of the most memorable trips of my life. As for the flies, I just let them walk all over my ears and eyeballs like everyone else does out there.

It's not just internal negativity that can interfere with a natural high, but external negativity—even from loved ones—that can bring you down. I remember doing a high school workshop at a conference at Glassboro College in New Jersey and one of the advisors told the group a story about skydiving. It was the perfect natural high story: it involved something incredibly challenging—yet fun; she took every precaution to ensure her safety, which involved hiring a highly experienced instructor; she experienced a rush of positive emotions so strong she couldn't wait to tell people about it as soon as it was over.

Her story was uplifting until she got to the part about how when she returned home, her husband "picked and picked" at her experience, putting the whole idea down, until she didn't want to talk about it anymore. Despite loving the natural high, she told us that she had never considered doing it again because of her husband's negativity.

There are so many things that can interfere with a great natural high. Sometimes the biggest roadblock for people is that you've got to put in some work to achieve the natural high. It can require effort and creativity, but the payoff can change your life in a hugely positive way. Maybe, after reading this book, you'll consider overcoming an obstacle that's prevented you from achieving a healthy natural high you've always dreamed about.

Try This: If you'd like to learn more about natural highs, check out a fantastic organization I'm partnering with called Natural High (www.naturalhigh.org). Its founder is Jon Sundt, who lost both of his brothers to substance abuse and then went on to become a huge success in the business world. I've met with

Jon and seen him speak. There is no doubt that the tragedy of losing his brothers became a catalyst to all the great things that have followed in his life. Jon's ability to turn a negative into a positive is remarkable. In 1996, he created Natural High to promote (you guessed it) natural highs to students in a way that's truly authentic. He's got celebrity interviews on the site with stars like Cassadee Pope, who won *The Voice* competition in 2012, and Tim Howard, the goalie from the U.S. national soccer team. The videos are well-produced and engaging; you'll love them. Plus, the site offers curriculum materials that your school can use for free. The goal is to encourage you to get involved and go beyond the videos and discover your own natural highs. And why not let your school administrators know about Natural High and get them involved too? In my opinion, every school should use these materials.

Pick Your Brain:
Laughter Versus Cocaine

In my opinion, natural highs are superior to chemical highs because they combine short-term pleasure with long-term benefit. In 2003, a team from Stanford University demonstrated that laughter activated the same brain regions as cocaine use.[8] Two of the areas of activation that laughter and cocaine shared in common were the nucleus accumbens and the amygdala. These areas, together with a third area—the ventral tegmental area—make up the brain's reward system. When activated, the neurons in the reward system release dopamine—yes, I know, "dope" is actually in the word. When dopamine is released in the brain it's like giving a biscuit to a dog—the brain is the dog here. The person feels pleasure from the dopamine, which is very rewarding, and they're motivated to do it again—whatever it is.

Over time, drug use damages the reward center of the brain because it's being forced to release dopamine based on the dose the drug user is giving it. Natural highs use the same brain area, but the amount of dopamine released during a natural high doesn't damage the brain tissue. Eventually, the person who uses drugs will have a decreased ability to get high, while the person pursuing natural highs will not.

More Facts: Evidence for Natural Highs

Research articles on the subject of prevention don't use the phrase "natural highs"—rather, they prefer the terms "alternative" or "substance-free" activities. These terms are similar in that they all describe activities that are healthy and enjoyable. There have been a number of studies over the past decade suggesting that college students who hold positive attitudes toward substance-free activities, and engage in them regularly, tend to drink less frequently.[9,10] In addition, when the number of substance-free activities—such as exercise and other creative events—are increased, there is an overall decrease in alcohol use on campus.[11]

In a 2006 study, college students who reported drinking regularly were asked which alternatives to drinking they would consider just as enjoyable.[12] These alternatives were rated on a four-point scale (0 = unpleasant/neutral to 4 = extremely pleasant), and the most highly rated responses from both genders included watching movies, playing a team sport, eating at restaurants, and creative activities. The best predictor of whether or not the activity was considered "as enjoyable as drinking" was if it included two or more peers or a romantic partner.

The conclusion I've drawn from studies like these is that students who have enjoyable, affordable, and convenient alternatives to drinking may be more likely to reduce their substance use. It seems logical that students who do not use are more likely to continue that pattern if they also have activities that they rate as highly enjoyable.

My conclusion is supported by findings from a National Institute of Alcohol Abuse and Alcoholism panel that concluded colleges should offer more alcohol-free options such as coffeehouses and movies, and expanded hours for student centers and gyms.[13]

The beauty of alternative activities is that they are not exclusive to college students. High schools, middle schools, and community groups can also offer similar alternatives—albeit with increased supervision. The key to creating events that will be rated as "enjoyable" is to empower young people to help create these events.

Students need to take an active role in planning so that they'll feel a true sense of ownership over the event, can plan activities that reflect their interests, and will show up. For a program to succeed, it also needs to be flexible and grow with the changing interests of the students.

Don't Be Afraid to Take a Stand

My roommate heard my idea for a drug-free group and thought,
"That's social suicide."
I just looked at him and said, "Jason, you haven't washed
your sheets in a year—I'm not listening to you."
—Matt Bellace

When I arrived at Bucknell University, there were two things to do at night: drink and tip cows. I'm kidding, if there was cow-tipping it would have been more fun! The party scene at Bucknell wasn't much different from most colleges, but at that time I didn't know it. I was amazed by the intensity of it all. Living in the dorm was like living in an alcoholic family.

As time went on, this atmosphere made me increasingly uncomfortable. In my mind, I was faced with a choice. Either I was going to change my school and transfer, or change my school and do something about the problem. After speaking with friends and family, I decided to stay and change my school from within.

That decision was the catalyst for the prevention group I founded at Bucknell in 1993 called C.A.L.V.I.N. & H.O.B.B.E.S. It stands for Creating A Lively Valuable Ingenious New Habit Of Being (at) Bucknell & Enjoying Sobriety. You probably would have guessed that though, right?

The organization was based on the simple idea of having fun substance-free. We didn't tell people how to live their lives. We just provided alternative late-night activities, such as bowling, bringing comedians to campus, and duct-taping people to walls.

The group grew quickly and drew media attention on campus. Within a year and a half, we had over 50 regular members and events every weekend of the school year. I don't think it was so much what we did, but the fact that we enjoyed doing it together that made the difference.

The defining moment for C&H came in 1994. A student was walking to class one morning and was hit and killed by a drunk driver while crossing the street. The entire campus was devastated by the news and trying to make sense of what happened. A few weeks later at a meeting of the Bucknell trustees (a.k.a., the guys with all the money) I made a plea for help. I asked the trustees to consider making prevention more legitimate on campus by giving us a home. Several weeks later, I picked up the school newspaper and read the headline "Calvin & Hobbes to Take Over Former Fraternity House."

The trustees approved a quarter of a million dollars to fix up a former fraternity house so C&H could live there. The fraternity was Sigma Phi Epsilon, which had closed due to drug and alcohol violations (shocker). I suspect the trustees wanted to send a message to other fraternity houses that they could be next. In 1996 we moved in, prompting a *US News & World Report* story to state, "How times have changed."[14]

Our house drew other national media attention and gave us tremendous visibility on campus. Years later, Bucknell president William "Bro" Adams wrote my graduate school letter of recommendation and said, "Among Mr. Bellace's important contributions, none was more noticeable or consequential than the creation of the revolutionary student social and residential organization C.A.L.V.I.N. & H.O.B.B.E.S."

What do you think would happen to a coed substance-free house on a college campus? You might suspect it would be buried in toilet paper or splattered with eggs within days, but nothing happened for some time. Then, one night at around eleven o'clock, I was in my room when I heard what sounded like a large group of people outside. I looked out my window and saw 40 naked dudes running toward the house! Yes, I counted. I thought they were going to destroy the house. What I didn't know was that it was the Bucknell cross-country team and running naked on campus once a year was their tradition. I don't know why. It was like hazing for everyone who watched.

I ran from my room thinking the dumbest thing I could ever think: "I'm going to stop them." OK, you don't stop 40 naked dudes. In fact, you don't stop one naked dude. If a naked guy runs into my place right now, he can do whatever he wants. Anyway, as I ran toward the front door, the first guy was running in. For some reason, I quickly got him in a headlock. The whole group stopped short and the guy I was holding said, "You're holding me and I'm naked!"

I didn't know what to say. I should have said, "What's up, nephew?" Instead I gave the guy a hip toss and he flew backwards into his teammates behind him. Awkward! I am definitely against homophobia. If you're homophobic I think you're ignorant. But in that moment, when the one naked athlete hit the other 39, homophobia happened right there. They were running around screaming, "We're naked!" and I was thinking, "Hilarious! I will write this in a book someday." No, honestly, I never imagined I would tell this story to anyone, but there *is* a moral.

I took a stand for C&H that night, but more importantly the group took a stand for natural highs on campus. We had a lot of help during the early years. The group's advisor, Bob Thomas, the coordinator of alcohol and other drug prevention at Bucknell, was a guiding force in helping us get off the ground. There were various professors and administrators who talked with me about their support for the group and the movement. There were also countless members of the group who sacrificed their time and energy to create a group that has lived on.

Today, Bucknell University is a much different place on the weekends. I suspect many students still drink and do drugs, but now there are options for those who want to be healthier. Bucknell has a late-night café, a dance club, and many other activities every weekend that are paid for by the student government, as well as several substance-free residence halls. I'd like to believe that C&H played a major role in influencing the decision to increase alternative activities at Bucknell.

In October 2011, the group celebrated its eighteenth birthday! That means there will be members in C&H that were born the year after I founded the group. Somehow this information makes me feel better when I find gray hair in yet another location on my body.

Over the years, C&H has gone through its share of ups and downs. The group has moved a few times from its original location, partly because the fraternity was allowed to recolonize. For almost twelve years (2000–2011), C&H lived in a house with a functional kitchen and as a result, weekly dinners became a big

C&H tradition. This may be C&H's greatest accomplishment, providing a much-needed sense of community on Bucknell's campus.

As I'm writing this, C&H is living in its fourth house since 1995. In October 2013, the group celebrated 20 years of providing the campus with substance-free social events and residential options. Twenty years! It's almost legal! While attending the celebration event, I was moved by how many lives had been positively affected by C&H. There were countless stories of how it improved the college experience for students. I heard about several weddings between members (one reception even featured a cake created to look like the C&H house), and there were some kids crawling around and walking the earth because their parents met through the group. I couldn't be more proud of what they've accomplished over two decades. It wildly exceeded my expectations! (Which, by the way, is a great recipe for happiness.)

One of the best outcomes of a speaking engagement is when students are so inspired by my program that they decide to start a group similar to C&H at their school. I've seen groups in middle schools, high schools, and colleges embrace the idea of natural highs and sponsor fun, substance-free events for their peers. Like anything else, there are varying degrees of success with these groups. The best example I've seen involves a friend named Dave Bratton who took an existing grant and used it to create three separate groups at three different colleges in Morris County, New Jersey, collectively dubbed New Social Engine or NSE—all based on the template of C&H. It's a brilliant idea to combine these groups, because they can sponsor huge events that bring everybody together, like first-run movie nights and trips to Funplex, an amusement and outdoor water park. Some of the events have drawn 600 students!

My speaking work has brought me to Canada several times. In 2013, I was invited to speak at the Algoma School District, which is way up in northern Ontario. To get to some of the schools, I had to take two flights and then drive through snow for five hours. It's so far, I got angry at them for living there. By no means do I want to offend anyone down south, but it seems like the colder the climate, the warmer the people. Maybe they just need my body heat!

One of the events was in Sault Ste. Marie (which, wackily

enough, is pronounced "Soo Saint Marie"), where I spoke to student leaders and vice principals. The district never had an alcohol or drug awareness week but after hearing my program, they decided to create an entire week at each school dedicated to natural highs. When I returned a year later and heard about it and all the different events they sponsored, I was blown away! They had snow-walk-a-thons, snow-skiing, and snow Olympics. I'm putting "snow" in front of all of these words, but up there they wouldn't bother. They laugh at me for saying "ice hockey." To them it's just "hockey." The "ice" is assumed.

Many other groups have come and gone over the years, but the movement remains strong. In fact, a recent article in the *Wall Street Journal* interviewed Brandon Busteed, a college alcohol prevention researcher who commented, "About 100 colleges and universities do a good job of supporting alcohol-free activities that are frequent, regular and entertaining enough to compete with drinking."

Students often ask me how I got started in professional speaking. It began partly as a result of C&H gaining national attention and local schools inviting me to come speak to their students. I was also very fortunate to have the support of the T.I.G.S. director, who gave me the opportunity to talk every year at events. My presentations back then weren't very good, but I was always passionate about my message.

It took me over a decade to find my comedic voice and to really understand how to engage students. It may have taken that long because I was so focused at the time on getting into a Ph.D. program. However, it turns out that my experience with C&H and prevention speaking played a role in the admissions process. When I applied for my doctorate in clinical psychology, the competition was fierce. I interviewed at a school where there were 200 applicants for four spots—and only 20 applicants were interviewed. In the interview, the professor looked at my resume and skipped right to the paragraph about C&H. He read it and said, "Wow, this must have been hard for you!"

I said to myself, "Yeah, there were forty naked dudes."

We bonded over the story and I got into that school—Drexel University. What I didn't tell you before was that I applied to seventeen Ph.D. programs over two years and only got into one. That was my only shot. When I got accepted, I was told by that same professor that the program needed students like me—students who weren't afraid to take a stand and try something different.

Taking a stand is one of the most important elements to leading a naturally high lifestyle. I hope for you that one day when you are in that moment when someone is sitting across the table and assessing you—"Do we want her for this school?" or "Do we want to give him this job?"—they can say, "Yes. We want you because you were not afraid. You were not afraid to speak out against injustice. You were not afraid to stand up and be a leader. And you were not afraid to go through the good pain."

You don't have to be the founder of a group or the president of something to be a great leader. You can start by being a leader in your own life—just being you and doing what's best for yourself, no matter what anyone else says. I believe you will find it empowering to take a stand, especially when you know you're doing the right thing. Of course, it's up to you.

Pick Your Brain:
Critical Periods

It's really important for people to learn how to socialize in healthy ways while they're young. If they don't, they can miss out on developing critical social skills. There is a well-known neuroscience experiment from 1977 that demonstrated a critical period for the development of vision. The researchers raised a monkey from birth to six months of age with one eyelid surgically shut.[15] The surgery prevented the monkey from seeing through that eye for six months. When the eye was opened it became clear to the scientists that the monkey couldn't see out of the eye and the blindness was irreversible.

The scientists later discovered that the reason the monkey was blind wasn't because anything happened to the eye, but rather the area of the brain controlling vision was underdeveloped. Further studies revealed that visual deprivation in monkeys for as little as one week during the first six months of life can permanently impair vision.[16] And it turns out that visual development in monkeys is similar to that in humans.

This particular experiment brought forth the idea of critical periods in brain development, and they apply to many different life functions in humans. The development of social skills, for example, is a product of the type of environment a person is exposed to while growing up. There have been cases of infants who were abandoned in the wild, presumably raised by animals, and later returned to civilized society. They are known as feral children, and despite their ability to learn certain skills they showed permanently impaired social skills and language development.[17] In the 1800s, a feral child, named Wild Peter, could never learn the value of money and was reported to be completely indifferent to it. This might sound like a nice attribute for a young person, but Wild Peter could never learn the value of money regardless of how much time was spent trying to teach him.

A more recent example involves the Harlow monkey studies of the 1960s. Two psychologists named Harry and Margaret Harlow conducted various studies in which they observed monkeys raised in isolation. They found that monkeys isolated for six to twelve months were physically healthy, but socially impaired. Their behavior often included crouching in the corner of their cages and rocking back and forth. This ritualistic behavior is similar to that which is seen in severely autistic children, and is believed to be a means for reducing anxiety. The isolated monkeys did not interact with other monkeys when given the chance. They didn't fight, play, or show any sexual attraction.

The authors concluded that a six-month period of isolation during the first eighteen months of life produced persistent and serious disturbances in behavior. In contrast, the isolation of an older animal for the same period of time didn't have the same devastating results. We've learned that there is something vulnerable about the developing brain in that social isolation during a critical period which can cause irreversible changes in development.[18]

If we expand this thinking to adolescent social development, it might help put the concept of substance abuse prevention into a new perspective. We know that the human brain is not fully developed until age 25.[19]

What's especially relevant to young people is that the last areas of the brain to develop are those that involve complex decision-making and social development. If you allow the average fifteen-year-old to spend weekends getting drunk or high, they'll likely developing coping skills that rely heavily on drugs. However, if you take the average fifteen-year-old and provide them with healthy ways to have fun, they're more likely to rely on those skills both now and later on in life.

Wrap-Up

The four basic elements of leading a naturally high lifestyle are:
- Leaning on healthy people for support
- Expressing your emotions in a healthy way
- Achieving natural highs every day, and
- Don't be afraid to take a stand.

These four points were created both from my experiences and from research on the protective factors against substance abuse. It is truly one of the highlights of my life that so many schools in so many places have invited me to deliver this message to their students, staff, and parents. I never imagined that talking about natural highs would provide me with a lifetime full of natural highs.

Chapter 2

Laughing, Smiling and Other Highs Better Than Cocaine

Your brain knows how to balance a natural high.
You will never hear "That movie was so funny
last night, I'm hungover."
—Matt Bellace

There are two forms of laughing natural highs: laughing, and making others laugh. The natural high of laughing can be such an intense experience it can make your face hurt. These are the kinds of laughs you get while watching your favorite comedian or staying up all night in middle school at a sleepover. If you've ever had this kind of natural high you know why stand-up comics refer to doing well on stage as "killing" or "destroying" the audience.

Laughing can also be a subtle experience, like when you see a funny cartoon that makes you smile. The Far Side cartoons always seem to do that for me, especially the one of the child entering a gifted school and pushing against a door that reads "Pull."

The other form of a laughing natural high comes from making others laugh. Early in his career, comedian Jerry Seinfeld said that making a large crowd of people laugh was "the best moment I've ever felt." Making people laugh and getting paid afterwards is amazing, but you don't need to be a professional comedian to feel the high of making others laugh. If you have a good sense of humor and decent timing you can take advantage of any life situation. For example, women love jokes about their weight, and bosses are dying to know what you think about their hair transplant. OK, I'm totally kidding here. Making people laugh is the best, but it's also a social risk so be careful.

When it comes to laughter, I believe that it is truly better to give than to receive. Prior to becoming a comedian, I usually only made people laugh unintentionally. For example, in college I made the mistake of telling my friends that I had a fear of feminine products, or "gyno-lotro-phobia" as I called it. Of course, one of them thought it would be funny to get one of those maxi pads and stick it on my leg.

In that moment of tension with everyone laughing at me, I started scraping at the pad with a paper cup and announced, "These things must really hurt when girls take them off." Looks of horror and amusement filled the faces of every female in the room. One of them said, "No, you idiot, they go on the other way!" I was like, "Yeah, I'm sure no one has ever messed that one up before."

When I lived in New York City and performed more at comedy clubs, I was fortunate to spend a lot of time hanging out with other comedians. Even when we'd go on the road, we'd call each other. We were like NYC cab drivers (without all the yelling and broken English). My favorite thing was doing impressions on each other's voicemail. Comedian Joe Matarese has left several brilliant impressions on my voicemail, including Rocky Balboa and former Phillies announcer Harry Kalas. And we both do Tony Soprano impressions and love calling each other in his voice. One time, I left a message as Tony asking Joe to stop whining about life on his podcast because "I'm in heaven and I'm *still* fat." The natural high for me was getting a call back from him telling me how hard he laughed.

Today, I spend a lot of time in the car with my kids listening to their music. It's mind-numbingly boring, but sometimes it's great for a laugh. This winter when the big song from *Frozen,* "Let It Go," was huge, my kids got into singing it. It also happened to be a brutal winter when everyone in my family got sick multiple times. During a bout with a head cold my son tried to sing "Let It Go" and sounded like he was dry-heaving each time he hit the highest note, "Go." It became an instant goof to sing any high note accompanied by the sound of retching. And one of the great things about kids is, if they laugh at a joke once, they'll laugh at it 50 times.

My wife is a great laugher, which I am very lucky for because I would hate to bomb for life. The one bit that gets her every time is when we are driving and I make up phony words to songs on the radio. Just like the voicemails, I make sure the lyrics contain a reference to something that happened recently in our lives. A song that lends itself perfectly to this is Josh Grobin's "You Raise Me Up." It is slow, predictable, and just annoying enough that she doesn't mind the interruption.

Try This: Pick your favorite song and try to come up with words that make fun of something or someone that bothered you recently. If you hit just one or two lines well, you'll get the intended effect. If you do it in front of friends and make it about them, it's even better. The key to the comedy, though, is to not make it sound mean. I know it can seem like mean is funny, but trust me—the second it sounds angry, people will not laugh.

Comedy = Pain + Time

The second time I auditioned at the Comic Strip Comedy Club in New York City, the judge came up to me afterwards and said, "You were better!" I said, "Wow, thanks!" She said, "No. Last time, you were better."
—Matt Bellace

In my opinion, the best laughing natural highs come from stressful situations. I think one reason humans evolved the ability to laugh was to counteract the natural lows that can happen in life sometimes. I know that many of my bits have come from my own low moments. For example, several years ago my wife went to her college reunion and returned home very upset. She said, "Matt, I don't know how to tell you this, but this weekend, I had feelings for my ex-boyfriend." I looked at her and said, "So? I had feelings for eight women today. Two were on TV, one was in an e-mail."

That joke is one of my favorites because it's so honest. It was actually a very painful experience to have her come home from a weekend away and share those feelings. It was not instant comedy, but once a few months had passed—and our relationship survived—it became fodder.

Time has a way of giving you a perspective on life. More importantly, if you're going to go through all that it takes to be a stand-up comedian, you had better believe in what you're saying. Talk about something that matters to you and something that moves you.

Laughter is also a great coping mechanism for dealing with life's little irritations. I remember being on a flight to San Francisco and was happy about getting the aisle seat. "It's quicker to the bathroom and easier to stick my legs out," I thought. What I didn't realize is that the aisle seat is five solid hours of people rubbing themselves on me like a bear marking a tree. It was like a butt parade on my shoulder. Just once I wish the airlines could produce an honest safety video saying, "We're sorry, but if you're sitting in an aisle seat you may be emotionally traumatized."

My favorite story of agitation in the air involved getting bumped up to first class. I know I'll get zero sympathy for flying in first class, but don't judge, because of course I am always grateful to be in an economy seat where I feel the arm hair of the guy sitting next to me. Anyway, on that day, I got to my luxurious first-class seat and the guy next to me was drinking alcohol like he was the pilot. I'm kidding, I love pilots and I know most are not like Denzel Washington in the movie *Flight*. So this guy had three empty little alcohol bottles on his tray and we were still on the ground. I wanted to lean in and say, "You don't need to drink. We're in first class. We're rock stars!" But I didn't. It was a cross-country flight and I knew there was going to be trouble.

Sure enough, an hour into the flight, the flight attendant came down the aisle to take our dinner order. It's weird on a plane to hear, "Will you be joining us for dinner?" How do you respond? "No, I have reservations in the bathroom." Of course, I'll be joining you! "What do you have?" She said, "We have chicken or shrimp." I ordered the chicken.

The stewardess turns to the guy next to me, and says, "Will you be joining us for dinner?" He agreed and she followed with "I'm sorry, we only have the shrimp left." Now a situation like this may not be a big deal to a lot of people, but Drunk Guy started yelling, "What? I wanted the chicken!" Visibly annoyed, the flight attendant says, "I'm sorry, I gave the last one away." Drunk Guy yells back, "I know, you gave it to this jerk right here!"

The whole thing was ridiculous, but then it got worse. The

guy across the aisle pipes up with "You're obnoxious! Settle down, man." Drunk Guy unbuckles, gets up, and says, "Want to take it outside?" We're at 30,000 feet and he wants to take it outside! That actually would have been fine with me. Honestly, it was the worst flight I ever had, but the best chicken.

Try This: Write down a painful or embarrassing life event that you are comfortable sharing with others. Don't write down every detail, just the most powerful elements. After a revealing statement consider adding a punch line. For example, "Getting dumped was the most painful moment of my life, like being forced to listen to Justin Bieber." Once you've got a solid story with a couple of punch lines, read it to a friend or post it online and see what other people think.

Pick Your Brain:
Laughter

A 2003 study—mentioned briefly in the first chapter—showed that laughing activated the same brain areas as cocaine.[1] I'm mentioning the study again because the findings are so important to the discussion of natural versus chemical highs that it's worth going into more detail. In addition, I believe that a deeper understanding of how this information is collected will allow you to make a more informed decision.

The study presented 42 "funny" and 42 "unfunny" cartoons drawn by Bizarro cartoonist Dan Piraro. One funny cartoon showed a man sitting on a deserted island looking malnourished and dirty with a bizarre creature sitting next to him. The caption—from the creature—read, "If I have to spend one more day on this island, I'm going to start hallucinating." Of course, you'd expect the man to be hallucinating about the creature, not the other way around, which makes the cartoon amusing. It's not exactly laugh-out-loud funny, but it generated a smile from me the first time I saw it.

The unfunny cartoon is the same man, except there's no creature and now the caption is coming from the man. There's really nothing remotely funny about the second one—it's simply a realistic thought.

These cartoons were shown to healthy volunteers while their brains were scanned in a functional MRI (fMRI) machine. Functional MRIs look just like regular MRI machines, but they contain software that measures changes in blood flow across brain tissue. While in the fMRI, participants were asked to press a button to indicate something as either "funny" or "unfunny." Comparing each person's "funny" brain scan to their "unfunny" brain scan, scientists were able to show that when something is perceived as funny, the reward center of the brain increases in blood flow. This is relevant because previous fMRI studies had also shown that the reward center increases blood flow activity during cocaine-induced highs.[2]

The knowledge about the reward center of the human brain comes mostly from research on the rat brain. The chemistry of the human brain and the rat brain are similar and it's believed that the process of drug addiction may be the same for both.

Laughter may not be more intense than a cocaine high, but I believe it's a better high than cocaine on many levels. The health benefits from laughter include improved immune functioning, stress relief, increased pain tolerance, and improved cardiovascular health.[3,4] For myself, I've gained psychological benefits from laughter, including reduced anxiety, bonding with other people in a shared experience, and improved mood. Interestingly, long-term cocaine use can have the opposite effect, including negative impacts on cardiovascular health as well as increased anxiety and stress.[5]

Getting the Joke

A girl called me up and said, "Rodney, come on over—there's nobody home."
I went over—nobody was home."
—Rodney Dangerfield

During my internship at Mount Sinai Medical Center, I created a workshop for traumatic brain injury patients to help them work on understanding humor. The participants had all been in rehabilitation for a year or more, but were still recovering. One of the lesser known effects of a traumatic brain injury is the loss of subtle cognitive skills, like understanding sarcasm and abstract humor. The joke above was one of the first I presented to the group and no one got it. So I asked, "What is this joke saying?" A female patient responded, "Well, he went over and no one was home." I said, "Yes, but why is that funny?" The blank stares made me realize that the patients had taken the joke literally. In their minds, no one was home because the girl said no one was home. They were thinking concretely about the joke because their ability to see another perspective was impaired.

The toughest part of receiving laughter is that you have to get the joke. The understanding of jokes has a mysterious quality to it. The brain is involved and it comes from one part intelligence, one part social awareness, and at least a little sense of humor.

I knew I had what it took from an early age because my second-grade teacher, Mrs. Marks, told my mother, "Matthew is the only student who gets all of my jokes." I was probably just an awful kiss-up from an early age, but at least I knew when to laugh.

You may not realize it, but there are unspoken social rules about laughter. I love Joe Pesci's famous scene in the movie *Goodfellas*. A recent search on YouTube titles this scene "Funny Guy." It takes place in a nightclub and all these mobsters are sitting around laughing out loud at Pesci's character, who is telling a funny story. Ray Liotta's character—in a very complimentary way—calls him a "funny guy." Pesci's mood quickly gets dark and he becomes belligerent toward Liotta's character. He repeatedly asks him in angrier and angrier tones, "You think I'm funny? What makes me so funny?"

The tension builds to the verge of violence until Pesci's character and the entire table erupts into laughter. The scene is so memorable partly because it violates our perception of what's supposed to happen when people are laughing. Evolutionary scientists believe that laughter evolved as a way to let the others in the group know that everything is safe. The *Goodfellas* scene does not turn violent. However, the mere suggestion of violence during a humorous moment is so unusual—yet fitting for antisocial criminals—that it instantly became part of American pop culture history.

I remember that in elementary school, it didn't require much to get a good laugh going. Of course, no one could blame a kid for being so happy back then because at any point during the school day you could play my favorite game—the parachute game. I recently watched kindergarten kids in a gym, standing in a circle and shaking the parachute really hard, and I thought, "No drug ever invented is better than shaking a parachute." When I was little we used to shake until someone passed out or a vertebrae popped out of our neck. My favorite part was when the teacher would say, "Someone run underneath." I had a friend with a sick sense of humor who once loudly suggested, "Hey, what about Timmy?" I said, "Doesn't Timmy have anxiety problems?" To which he just looked at me and nodded and I thought, "Poor Timmy."

In middle school, all I needed for a great laugh were my friends and a sleepover. Take some pizza, add a little sleep deprivation, and somehow the comedian in all of us was magically unlocked. Suddenly, around 3 AM everything was hilarious. Everyone could be laughing and you'd hear, "But I *did* drop the table on my toe!" The laughter would just get louder. It was almost like our brains hit a point where they could relax and find the funny in almost every situation.

Try This: Plan an old-school sleepover with friends. If you think you're too old for it then try a road trip, an outdoor adventure weekend, or a vacation house. It doesn't matter what you do, just make sure it involves hanging out late at night with good friends and see if you can have a laughing natural high.

Interview with Comedians: Getting the Joke

In preparing this chapter, I interviewed a few of New York City's finest comedians about their first experiences watching stand-up comedy. All of them reported that it took place while they were young and it obviously had a profound effect on their choice of profession. The comedians I spoke to were Ted Alexandro, who's appeared on *Late Show with David Letterman*, Conan O'Brien, and *Comedy Central Presents*; Dave Siegel, who's appeared on Comedy Central's *Laugh Riots*; Moody McCarthy, who's appeared on *Last Comic Standing* and *Jimmy Kimmel Live*; and Joe Matarese, who's appeared on *Late Show with David Letterman* and *Comedy Central Presents*.

Ted Alexandro

"As a kid, I listened to all of my parents' comedy albums. It was such an intimate experience because there was no image to watch—just sound to engage my entire imagination. It was so appealing to me—not just the laughter, but the pauses. Here was this person who was speaking to a room full of people, commanding their attention to the point where they would listen intently even when he wasn't being funny. The comic that stands out the most early on was Steve Martin, but in high school it was Eddie Murphy."

Dave Siegel

"I grew up in Woodmere, New York, on Long Island. In the summer, my parents would take me to the Westbury Music Fair. I remember watching Rodney Dangerfield and Jackie Mason perform. I'm sure most of their jokes went over my head, but I remember seeing a bit about baseball players adjusting their crotch at home plate. As a huge baseball fan I completely related to it and laughed hysterically. It was so good that as soon as I got home I had to immediately start telling my friends the joke."

Moody McCarthy

"It was while watching Richard Pryor tapes and seeing the guy totally in command of a large group of people. I was twelve years old—didn't get all of the jokes—but had fun watching my brothers being in awe of him. It was also completely intimidating to watch Pryor. I never thought, 'I could do that.'"

Joe Matarese

"I guess like a lot of comics my age, it was listening to Steve Martin. I grew up in Cherry Hill, New Jersey, and was about eleven or twelve when I would get together with a neighbor and listen to albums in the basement. Listening to stand-up comedians also became a way for me to connect with my father. Listening to albums together would help me feel closer to him—I still do it today, but now it's with clips on YouTube."

Making Others Laugh

The four levels of comedy: Make your friends laugh,
make strangers laugh,
get paid to make strangers laugh,
and make people talk like you because it's so much fun.
—Jerry Seinfeld, during an interview

Do you think you're funny? Do you believe you could get up and make a room full of people laugh? The philosophy of the Manhattan Comedy School in New York City is that anyone can learn stand-up comedy and perform a five-minute set. I agree. Andy Engel, its founder, runs the school out of Gotham Comedy Club and takes students from their first joke to a performance at a comedy club. Comedy classes are truly the first rung on the entertainment ladder, but I know from experience that they can be a lot of fun.

One benefit of taking a comedy class is social support. The environment of comedy classes tends to be very supportive, which is what you'll need to combat the full-on self-esteem assault known as stand-up comedy. One of the most supportive experiences I ever had in my life occurred as a result of taking a stand-up comedy class at Camden Community College in Black-wood, New Jersey.

The final exam was a performance at a hole-in-the-wall "comedy club" called Bonkers Comedy Café. The place actually had a four-foot hole in the wall behind the stage that led to a huge room below. If you leaned against the curtain the wrong way, you could fall 30 feet down onto rubble. It would have been a great show if any comic who bombed got pushed through the hole.

My favorite memory of the whole night was the intro music that our so-called teacher (who wasn't even remotely funny) played before each act. It was Eddie Money's cheesy 1980s song "Think I'm in Love." Do yourself a favor and either download a 30-second free clip of this miserable song or check out the song during the ending credits of the Kevin James movie *Paul Blart: Mall Cop*.

Imagine eight comedians—introduced one after the other—and then start and stop the song mid-lyric. The guy never even bothered to restart the song, so you would just hear "Give it up for your next-up comedian, Vince Valentine" and then "I think I'm in love, and my life's—" and then Vince would begin his set.

My classmates and I were all so nervous about performing for the first time that none of us even acknowledged the hole, the rubble below, or the lame music. Our anxiety was understandable since we were performing in front of our friends and family. I know veteran comics who still get nervous performing in front of their loved ones. However, the experience bonded us because there was this sense that we were all in it together. That's my favorite part of performing stand-up comedy in New York City: the sense of community. It may sound silly, but this feeling of support in the class freed me to try jokes that I otherwise wouldn't have attempted.

It's been more than seven years since the class, but I still keep in touch with two of my fellow classmates. One of them is Caroline, a mother of three who took the class to try something new. To be honest, when I first met her she seemed fairly depressed. She was also so nervous the first time she stood up to perform in class, it made me uncomfortable.

But over the eight-week course, Caroline underwent a transformation. There was something about the support of strangers and the high of getting laughs that seemed to motivate her. By the night of the performance, she had lost weight, was more confident, and when she got on stage, she blew us away! Not only was she funny, but inspirational as well.

Several years later, Caroline wrote to me and told me about her battle with a brain tumor. She was recovering and wanted to return to stand-up to try to recapture some of those great feelings. I was so honored that she had taken the time to get in touch with me and share her story. We only knew each other for a couple of months, but the bond had remained. In her mind, I was a positive and supportive influence at a crucial time in her life.

We all need those people we can turn to for unconditional support, but it feels even better to be one of those people who can provide the unconditional support.

Try This: If you're interested in becoming a comedian, try taking a comedy workshop or improvisation class near you. If you live close to New York City, I recommend Andy Engel's Manhattan Comedy School (www.manhattancomedyschool.com). If you live near Philadelphia, I recommend the Philadelphia Comedy Academy (www.philadelphiacomedyacademy.com). If you live elsewhere, just do a search for comedy clubs in your area. There's likely a decent chance that they offer classes or at least an open mike session.

Classes tend to be a commitment of several weeks and two or three hundred dollars. It'll definitely expand your horizons, improve your speaking skills, and give you a safe environment in which to perform. During the class, you can also really experience the natural high of giving laughter and receiving laughter. You may even make some friends in the process.

For the Love of the Game

The hardest part of traveling the country and making others laugh is the uncertainty of the career. No one can tell you how long it will take to become a successful comedian—or even if it will ever happen. When I started doing comedy, I remember rushing home from my psychology job, skipping dinner, and quickly getting dressed so I could pay to perform at an open mike. My wife asked me, "Why are you doing this to yourself?" I just looked at her said, "You're right. I should quit psychology."

I consider myself extremely fortunate. My career has been described as a "hybrid"; I get to tell jokes, but also get to motivate students in the process. On a good day, I feel like my work brings me unparalleled fulfillment. It also happens to be a lot more stable than performing at the Ha Ha Hole. Don't get me wrong, performing in comedy clubs is fun. As Jerry Seinfeld has said, they're like a "sweaty gym" where jokes are worked out. However, the lifestyle of late nights, alcohol and drug use, and other risky behaviors can be deadly for some comedians. As the psychologist in the green room, I spent a lot of nights giving free therapy between shows.

One of the keys to living naturally high in your life—no matter what your career—is having a passion for what you do. It's a lot more difficult to get into trouble when you're focused on working hard and accomplishing things. The great thing about comedy is there's a never-ending amount of work to be done.

Your act is never "finished"—there are always more jokes to be written, more exploration to be done. As I look back at my very early days of trying to make people laugh, I realize that my work was beginning long before I ever stepped on stage.

One problem I had to overcome before I could do comedy was convincing others that what I was saying was meant to be funny—not mean. The first thing I had to realize was that my facial expressions were always the same when telling a joke. That's fine if you're Steven Wright or Norm Macdonald, but I was not. My straight-faced delivery would leave some people looking at me and thinking, "Wow, what a jerk!"

Fortunately, a friend of mine clued me into this—of course, I felt horrible because I was just trying to be funny. So, as I learned more about the finer points of comedy, I began making my punch lines more obvious with a slight change in my tone of voice or an exaggerated facial expression. Things improved very quickly. It was a turning point for me because you always have to "sell" the joke, which means you have to subtly indicate that you are kidding.

I also learned not to rely on jokes that attack people, especially those with physical or mental problems. I remember when I was five years old, I asked this large man, "Why are you so fat?" He was so nice about it, too. He didn't get upset. If I was him, I probably would have responded, "Because five-year-olds are so delicious."

Honestly, I was probably just mimicking the negative things I heard about overweight people while growing up around my dad. Recently, we were standing outside of Cold Stone Creamery when he said, "Look at those people eat all that fat!" He remarked, shaking his head, "Isn't that something?" I was like, "Yeah, Dad, it's called happiness."

By seventh grade, I still hadn't learned my lesson. I got caught in history class drawing a cartoon mocking a classmate named CJ, who spent a lot of time hitting on girls in our class. By midyear, he must have asked out half the girls in our grade and it wasn't because he was so good at it. The cartoon happened to be pretty funny, but the real problem was that our history teacher happened to be CJ's mother. I can still remember the feeling I got as she swiped the cartoon out of my hand. To her credit, she remained fairly calm, but I felt like I had just kidnapped her child. I had no one to blame. It was my fault and I was being mean. It was a lesson that I still remember to this day—there are actually rules in comedy.

For those who love comedy so much they wish to pursue it as a career, there are many paths the career can take. This chapter focused heavily on stand-up, but there's also comedic acting like in sketch comedy or improvisation. Many comedians go on to become writers for television talk shows and sitcoms. For those lucky enough to make it as performers on television, the sky's the limit. Comedy has launched the careers of so many television and movie stars over the years, including Jerry Seinfeld, Eddie Murphy, Jim Carrey, Kevin James, and Chris Rock.

I love stand-up comedy more now than ever. I appreciate and support comedians who do it well. And in recent years, colleges, high schools, and community groups have asked me to do comedy shows in the evenings. For example, the Municipal Alliance of Morris County, New Jersey, hosted me for a day of speaking programs followed by an evening "natural high comedy event." What great synergy. I got to carry over my message beyond the school day *and* there was funding to bring out a couple of my fellow comedian friends to perform with me. The only difference between a typical comedy show in a club and one of these "natural high" events is that the comedians are a bit cleaner and don't glamorize alcohol or other drug abuse to get laughs.

In recent years, the comedy community has lost a number of phenomenally talented comedians, who just plain died too young. Robin Williams was the most famous. From the news reports, Williams admitted to abusing alcohol and cocaine for many years and entered rehab several times. After he committed suicide, his wife announced that he was suffering from Parkinson's disease. This is a condition caused by degeneration of the neurons in the brain, which results in serious problems in movement and mood, to name just a few. Any neuroscientist will tell you that cocaine abuse puts people at risk for Parkinson's, which could lead to severe depression and possibly suicide. In my opinion, drug use contributed to the death of this supremely gifted comedian. Unfortunately, he wasn't the first and I don't think he will be the last.

Natural High Event Idea: Consider putting on a natural high comedy night in your area. They're really fun! It could be a show for students, adults, or both. You can hold it in a local comedy club and let the staff run it, or you can find the comedians yourself. This may sound difficult, but thanks to the internet comedians can be viewed and booked online. Just make sure you pick comedians who are comfortable doing cleaner material.

Wrap-Up

Laughter is a natural high produced by the brain to help you feel better and safer about the world. People of all ages can benefit from the physical and psychological effects of laughter. Laughing releases a neurotransmitter—a brain chemical—called dopamine in the reward center of the brain and gives a sense of euphoria. The brain releases many neurotransmitters, but the main role of dopamine is to be the "feel good" chemical. If you love the natural high of laughter, you may wish to pursue it as a career in stand-up or comedic acting. It's not easy, but at least there are a lot of laughs along the way.

Chapter 3

Running, Surfing and Other Highs Better Than Weed

You have to stay in shape. My grandmother started walking five miles a day when she turned 60. She's 97 today and we don't know where she is.
—Ellen DeGeneres

In eighth grade I used to wake up at 6 AM and run three miles before school. It was self-inflicted torture—like making your own bed at a hotel. Any dedicated runner would probably call my routine a day off, but I was in training to be the greatest middle school athlete the world had ever seen. Unfortunately, there was no award for a young athlete with shockingly large eyebrows or I would have won hands-down.

My morning runs were a natural high. I can still remember how great it felt in class on the mornings I ran. My mood was more positive and my energy level was through the roof. I actually had a better attitude about doing schoolwork. My mindset toward school back then, to paraphrase comedian Joe Matarese, was "I don't need math, I'll just use a calculator. I don't need to read, I'll just be quiet." But something about having more energy in class makes you feel like you can do anything.

As an athlete in high school, however, running was served up as punishment for a bad performance. We only ran when we were forced to, so I avoided it. In graduate school, I rediscovered running for pleasure because I was too poor to join a gym and in need of a healthy coping mechanism to deal with stress. I met my soon-to-be wife in graduate school and she is a real runner. She was on the cross country and track teams at Colgate University and even today can run for ten miles at around a six-minute pace per mile. She runs almost every day during all seasons. She has a saying: "There's no such thing as bad weather, just bad clothing."

I used to think my wife was crazy for running in the winter. I had a dozen reasons why I would never do it. I used to think it was bad to run in the cold until I read that humans can tolerate running in freezing cold much better than they can in sizzling hot conditions. I used to think that running while sick was ridiculous until I read that as long as you don't have a respiratory infection or the flu, running actually makes you feel better even if it doesn't improve the condition.

My relationship with running has changed significantly over the years. Following my knee surgery, I was instructed not to run because the cartilage in my knee is now mostly scar tissue and doesn't respond well to the pounding. It's part of the human condition to lose abilities and be forced to adapt. Fortunately, I've discovered other activities that give me a similar natural high. Biking outside, swimming, gardening, and even just going for a walk improves my mood. I look at fitness as being just as much about improving my mental health as it is about maintaining my physical health. When I used to live in New York City, I remember seeing a guy in Central Park using an apparatus that was a hybrid of a bike and an elliptical machine. He was powering over the hills while standing up like a runner, but moving with the speed of a biker. That's the kind of adventurous spirit we all could benefit from!

One of the most important elements to achieving natural highs is to keep an open mind. Ultimately, enjoying life is about positive risk-taking. Aleta Meyer, a prevention expert from the National Institute on Drug Abuse, stresses the importance of positive risk-taking for healthy development. She feels that without constructive challenges, young people will fulfill their risk-taking needs by turning to substance abuse or unhealthy natural highs like speeding in a car or high-risk sexual activity. The brain goes through an intense period of learning during adolescence and learning means trying new things and taking risks. For teens, the question is not are they taking risks, but rather what risks are they taking? The young person experimenting with drugs is still intensely learning, but they're learning something potentially destructive. It's important to encourage young people to take on positive risks through activities like sports, trying out for the school play, learning to cook, or building something that pushes personal limits and helps fulfill emotional needs.

Interviews with Runners

As a guy with perpetual knee problems, I'm not the best to comment on the runner's high. To learn more about it, I reached out to my support network and received help from those nearest and dearest to me who do run. It may surprise you to learn that all of them reported achieving the runner's high, but what it takes them to get it varied. Moody McCarthy is a comedian mentioned above and longtime runner, Dara Bellace is my wife and a former Division I cross-country runner, and Katie Heineken is a runner with five marathons under her belt (and the ironic name in a book like this).

Moody McCarthy

"I've definitely had the runner's high. It's that feeling you get after a few miles when you actually feel better. It is counterintuitive to feel better! As a comedian, I would say that comedy is a better high though—probably because I can't make a living as a runner."

Dara Bellace

"Running allows me to feel free and strong. It's very empowering to just get away from it all and get outside for a run. After a long run, I feel accomplished and drained, and enjoy a good kind of soreness. I also feel more productive when I return to work. Even if I can run for just twenty-five minutes, I feel more energized and clearheaded. A run on a crisp twenty-degree day in Central Park is my natural high. I don't need a beer or anything like that."

Katie Heineken

"I have had natural highs from running, but it's not the same since I started running marathons. In the New York City Marathon, I got one while crossing the Queensboro Bridge, entering Manhattan, and hearing everyone cheering. In general, running helps me focus more at work; it also gives me a sense of accomplishment (and a great appetite). I also love how it feels to take a shower after a run. I feel cleaner for some reason."

Try This: New Year's Eve in Motion

One of my favorite New Year's Eve events to promote is the official Midnight Run through Central Park in New York City. New Year's Eve has become synonymous with getting chemically high, so what better way to be a nonconformist than to go for a run? The race kicks off with fireworks as the ball drops and the atmosphere is more of a party than a race. There are costumes, dancing, and lots of noisemakers—like a cross between Halloween and a World Cup soccer match. For more information, check out www.nyrr.org.

Honestly, I don't like hanging out in New York City on New Year's Eve. I've come to prefer the skiing and snowboarding scene in the mountains. There are many slopes that stay open at night for skiing under the lights. For those of you who live close enough to a mountain with night skiing, it's worth trying even if you're only good enough for the bunny hill. It will change your brain chemistry in a positive way to be active late at night and you'll feel like you're moving twice as fast in the dark!

If you're someone who dislikes the typical New Year's Eve celebrations—or any event focused entirely on drinking and doing drugs—then give yourself permission to just leave and do something else. For those in recovery, it's important way to help maintain your sobriety. For those in school who play competitive sports, it will be one less potential obstacle to playing (and playing well). For those who have a mother who would kill you for coming home drunk or high, it's one less thing that could end your life. I've found that midnight runs, late-night movies, stand-up comedy shows, hanging out with like-minded friends, and playing video games are all infinitely better than hanging around someplace pretending I'm having fun.

The Running Cure

One of the greatest things about running in Central Park is the opportunity to see so many different people. Achilles, a worldwide organization that enables people with all types of disabilities to participate in athletics, is one of the most prominent groups in the park. If you arrive at the right time on a Saturday or Sunday morning at the 90th and Fifth Avenue entrance to Central Park, you'll see Achilles members preparing their wheelchairs for exercise. These aren't typical wheelchairs. They are the Orange County Choppers of wheelchairs. They have chairs you can pedal with your hands, chairs with chrome wheels, and even chairs that allow you to lie completely flat.

My favorite is the guy who goes out in a basic old wheelchair. He doesn't look impressive until he starts up a big hill. I have seen this guy at least a dozen times pushing himself uphill—in reverse! I don't care how lazy or down I'm feeling that day; seeing him motivates me to keep going.

The other running group in Central Park that always fascinates me is a group from Odyssey House. These are individuals in recovery from substance abuse who are taking part in an innovative treatment community. Odyssey House uses running to encourage former heroin, cocaine, and crack addicts to stay clean.

The whole thing sounded like a bit from my stand-up act until I started reading about these folks and the science behind what they're doing. [1-3] And, of course, the first time I watched an Odyssey House guy run by me I didn't think it was a joke anymore. I shouldn't have assumed that my clean liver would give me breakaway speed.

Odyssey House has produced some serious runners. In fact, they routinely enter around fifteen people into the New York City Marathon each fall.

The use of running, or any activity that increases heart rate for more than 30 minutes, to treat addiction has received increasing amounts of attention from researchers. A study conducted at Butler Hospital in Rhode Island found that outpatient treatment for alcoholism that included twelve weeks of aerobic conditioning increased the likelihood of remaining sober.[2] This makes sense given that endurance training has been shown to have a variety of positive psychological effects, including stress reduction, improved mood, and reduced pain perception. In a sense, the runner's high can replace chemical highs while acting as a healthier coping mechanism for stress.

Try This: If you have some time, read about the history and innovative treatment going on at Odyssey House. It all began in 1966 as a pilot research program at Metropolitan Hospital in New York City. They started out treating heroin abusers and quickly grew into one of the country's first drug-free therapeutic communities. For more information, go to www.odysseyhouseinc.org.

Pick Your Brain:
The Runner's High

"Runner's high" sounds like an oxymoron. How can you get a high from doing something that causes you pain? But it's true! From my own experience and also talking with runners I know, there are really two versions of the high. There's the classic version where you run for a few miles, get through the initial pain, and then experience a euphoria that makes you think you can keep running forever. There's also a less dramatic runner's high that's very satisfying, too. It's the high that follows a run, which includes a sense of accomplishment, relaxation, increased ability to focus, and improved mood. This kind of high can last for hours or even days. Running is one of those activities that will cost you time and a little bit of money for a decent pair of shoes, but will return so many benefits. Not a runner? Think about giving it a try. A lot of people like to run with a friend (or friends), so it can be a social thing as well. And running's not the only way to enjoy all these amazing benefits. Any form of cardio that gets your heart rate up, especially outdoors, will provide that natural high.

In the 1980s, a study showed that vigorous physical activity causes a release of endorphins from the brain into the bloodstream. For years, scientists just assumed that somehow those endorphins—which come from the brain's pituitary gland—made their way back to the brain and created a sensation of euphoria. It turns out that this assumption was not correct.

In a recent study, neuroscientists were able to demonstrate that the endorphins released by the pituitary gland don't return to the brain once they've been released into the body.[3] The reason they don't make it back is because of the blood-brain barrier, which acts like a screen to prevent large molecules from passing from the blood supply in the body to the blood supply of the brain. So if the pituitary endorphins aren't able to make it back to the brain, then what's causing the runner's high?

The study suggested that endorphins released locally (that is, from the cortex of the brain) could be binding to opioid receptors in the frontal lobe and limbic system of the brain.[3] If this were true, it would mean that the brain was releasing neurotransmitters for the primary reason of creating the sensation of euphoria. Competing research suggests that endorphins are not responsible for the runner's high, but rather a different chemical altogether.

I recently came across a study that showed that the runner's high activates the same brain receptors as marijuana.[4] The experiment had people in three groups: running, cycling, and couch potatoes. The runners and cyclists exercised at moderate levels (70–80% of maximum heart rate) for 45 minutes, and the couch potatoes sat for the same period of time. Blood was collected from all the participants immediately prior to and following each session.

Analysis of the exercisers' blood revealed significantly higher levels of anandamide—a neurotransmitter that binds to cannabinoid receptors in the brain—in post-exercise blood samples when compared to the pre-exercise blood samples. By the way, the couch potatoes' blood showed no change in anandamide levels.

What does this mean? Well, as its name implies, the cannabinoid receptor is sensitive to THC, the active ingredient in cannabis (pot). When a person runs or does any activity that elevates their heart rate at a moderate level they're tapping into the same neurotransmitter system that is activated by smoking pot. This makes sense; the self-reported "positive" sensations of smoking pot and running are very similar—a reduction in pain, elevation in mood, and increased feeling of well-being.

One main difference between the pot high and the runner's high comes from research on memory functioning. A 2008 study showed heavy pot smoking (defined as five or more joints a week) decreases the volume of the hippocampus—a brain structure necessary for memory formation.[5] A smaller hippocampus has been shown to result in decreased memory functioning, while exercise has been shown to have the exact opposite effect—it actually increases hippocampal volume and improves memory functioning.[6]

I remember presenting this information to a small group of private school students outside of Washington, D.C., and one student seemed particularly concerned. He said to me, "I've got ADHD and take Ritalin all week to focus, and on the weekend I smoke pot."

"Wow," I answered, "so you're telling me that your fifteen-year-old brain is exposed to a drug almost every day of your life?"

He responded, "Do you think I should get off the Ritalin?"

It was one of those moments in life where I wanted to laugh, but didn't want to encourage his behavior. I read about a psychiatrist in California who gave a teenager a prescription for medical marijuana because he thought the side effects were no worse than Ritalin. His license was revoked and he's probably in jail, but it's all the same thinking. People cringe at the thought of giving a fetus alcohol for good reason since their brains are so vulnerable. However, the fifteen-year-old brain is nearly a decade from being completely developed and exposing it to mind-altering substances is just as cringe-worthy. The research suggests that exploring natural options like regular exercise, better sleep, and good nutrition can improve focus and mood as much as any prescription drug.

The Runner's High, Legal in All 50 States

Cannabis always made me paranoid; I felt like people were watching me. And now I'm sober, and I've got this talk show in the middle of the night on CBS, and I now know that no one is watching me.
—Craig Ferguson

This chapter would feel incomplete without mentioning the national conversation on the legalization of marijuana for recreational use. In January of 2014, Colorado became the first state to legalize recreational use of the drug, followed a few months later by Washington state. This book is not the appropriate place to rehash the entire legal and political debate on the issue, especially with the passionate arguments from both sides that could fill hundreds of pages! However, I've found that there are several important points consistently missing from the debates, and they're all related to the impact on young people and their developing brains.

I perform regularly at drug-rehabilitation centers. At almost every gig I've done at a rehab, I'll hear stories from the staff about how much progress the young people make while they're there. They experience huge academic improvement in just a few months, and they often make a ton of social and emotional advances as well. Then they return home, often to the same environment that gave rise to their problems. If the students don't learn healthy coping mechanisms during rehab, they're doomed to fall back into their unhealthy behaviors. Unfortunately, I hear far too many of those stories too. I've seen it over and over again.

Pro-legalization people argue that regulation of marijuana will keep it out of the hands of young people. But this isn't a logical premise; it's well-known that regulation of alcohol hasn't kept it away from teens in any significant way. Cigarettes smoking among teens is at an all-time low, which is great. Warning labels have certainly helped. Certain regulations, like outlawing smoking in public places, have also helped (it's hard to look cool when you're smoking outside in the rain and are dripping wet). What's troubling me is that despite the progress made with cigarettes, there there's been an increase in teen use of marijuana over the last ten years. This is believed to be due to the increased accessibility of medical marijuana, and a reduction in the number of teens viewing the drug as harmful, according to the Monitoring the Future data from 2012. As I see it, the real issue for young people isn't about the legalization of another drug, it's about living in an environment that supports healthy choices.

So how do you make those healthy choices? One of the most important elements for success in life, both now and in the future, is learning how to regulate your own behavior. It's not always easy, and growing up in an environment that supports *unhealthy* ways to cope with stress—such as taking drugs, drinking alcohol, and/or engaging in violence—can make it even harder. My message of natural highs is essentially about being a leader in your own life: about making thoughtful decisions about how you respond to stress and how you decide to have fun. With increased access to recreational drugs, it may be that finding a healthy environment can get harder and harder. But it *is* possible.

A word about research. There's no such thing as the "perfect" study; science is all about looking at an experiment that worked once and testing it again and again until many people are confident that the results are real. In many cases, like studies on diet and health, the research goes back and forth on an issue for decades. In the case of cigarettes, tobacco companies—who had a strong financial interest in keeping people buying their product—argued for years that smoking was only "correlated" with lung cancer and did not "cause" lung cancer. Eventually, enough of these correlational studies were done, and finally scientists and the public accepted it: smoking causes lung cancer. Research on marijuana is still in the early stages, but it feels a lot like those early days of cigarette research. Look at any comment section of an online article about how marijuana negatively impacts brain development and you'll likely see stuff like "Correlation is not causation." I urge you to keep in mind that this argument may not hold up forever. And I also suggest you take a hard look at who's making money from the sale of marijuana.

After one of my parent programs, a mom and dad approached me and said they were very worried about their sixteen-year-old son. He was starting to hang out with friends who took lots of negative risks and they saw a sudden decrease in his motivation to do homework, play sports, or do anything productive. They had recently found evidence that he was using pot and they confronted him. He denied it, but they didn't believe him. Lack of motivation is common among teenagers, but with an onset so rapid, it suggests a more neurological basis for the emotional change.

The National Institute of Drug Abuse in Bethesda, Maryland, coordinated a study of young adults that examined how marijuana impacts the emotional state of regular users.[7] The study looked at two groups, regular marijuana users and non-marijuana users, after they received an amphetamine-type drug that produces an "up" feeling. The brains of regular marijuana users reacted differently to the amphetamine-type drug, including a significantly smaller "up" feeling when compared to the other group. In addition, among the regular marijuana users, there was a decreased response in the part of the brain that releases the feel-good chemical dopamine. The authors concluded that this might be the basis for the "amotivational syndrome" seen so frequently in teenagers who regularly smoke pot. In everyday terms, this might mean quitting that sport you love because you suddenly think it's stupid or a waste of time. Your drug-free mind would never have come to that conclusion, but this study suggests smoking marijuana regularly could create that type of thinking.

The pro-legalization movement displays a lot of empathy for parents with small children who have rare conditions, like epilepsy or chronic pain. That's great, but we also need to have empathy for the parents of the millions of teens who are smoking pot regularly and failing in school. And we need to have empathy for the millions of teens who've been sold this lie that marijuana is harmless and won't impact your life.

To give you some insight into this particular issue, you should know that there's not much good research in the U.S. on the effectiveness of medical marijuana in treating those rare medical conditions. I do hope that changes soon. However, there is mounting evidence *right now* about the negative impact of marijuana on the teen brain and in my opinion, it doesn't get enough publicity.

If you don't have a college degree in this country, you're giving up over $500,000 of lifetime income.[8] Research indicates that the more marijuana a young person consumes between ages fourteen and twenty-five, the lower his or her chances of getting a college degree.[9] A recent study from Australia showed that smoking marijuana daily increased the odds of not graduating from high school or college by 60%.[10] There are a lot of different ways in which a person can do poorly in school, but using marijuana actually seems to make it more likely to happen.

So now you're learned about the connection between regular pot use and lowered motivation. Here's an even bigger problem: reduction of IQ. IQ stands for "intelligence quotient" and it's basically a number that, based on a test, compares how mentally quick and bright you are compared to other people your age. Of course, we all want to have the highest level of intelligence possible, and while it's not the only thing you need to be successful in life, it *does* matter. Your IQ stays fairly stable throughout your life, so your score at age 16 will be similar to your score at age 66—unless circumstances intervene.

The most well-constructed study I've ever read on marijuana

looked at how the drug impacted IQ across a person's lifespan.[11] Researchers started with over a thousand twelve-year-olds, none of whom had ever smoked pot, and gave them all IQ tests. Then the researchers continued to study them until they were 38 years old and gave them another IQ test. During the years in between, they asked all sorts of questions about the use of drugs, mental illness, and other events going on in their lives. The study found that among those who started smoking pot regularly as a teenager and continued until age 38, they lost up to eight IQ points.

I don't know about you, but I don't have many IQ points to be giving away. During my doctoral training, I monitored a lot of IQ tests, so I can tell you that a quick way to lower your IQ score is to lower your brain's processing speed. Just like a computer, your brain processes information at a certain speed. If your processing speed is slow, it can lower your score on the IQ test. There are a number of things that can lower your processing speed, including a head injury, depression, or drug use. In the study I described above, researchers found that reduced cognitive performance, including slower processing speed, was seen among the regular marijuana users.

I've met thousands of students across the country, and I can tell you that among them are young people who feel that they're entitled to a college degree, like it's a right guaranteed by the Constitution. There are some who have so much money or family influence that not graduating was never an option. To these students, I don't think the concept of losing IQ points will make much of a difference (although it should). But I hope all the other young people—the ones who don't see the world as "owing" them a degree—will hear my message. They want to achieve great things, they want to do it on their own, and they don't want anything to stand in their way. There are some students I meet who could be the first in their family to graduate college. To students like this, smoking pot is simply not worth it.

I've heard and read countless times, "Pot has never killed anyone in recorded history!" I imagine anyone involved in science education crying whenever they hear such an absolute statement. While it's true that the low concentration of THC in marijuana of the past produced few major side effects, the increased concentrations of THC in marijuana today, especially in the edible forms, has caused a number of heart-attack deaths. THC increases heart rate for up to six hours after ingestion and a person has a four times greater risk of a heart attack while under the influence. "Pot has never killed anyone"? Tell that to the families of the thousands of people who die every year while driving a vehicle under the influence of marijuana. Tell that to the parents of young NASCAR driver Kevin Ward, Jr., who had high levels of THC in his system when he decided to get out of his car during a race and was hit and killed by another driver. None of this makes pot the worst drug on the planet, but it also doesn't make it incapable of killing someone.

There's yet another troubling issue here: how mental illness is associated with marijuana use.

As a society we're comfortable joking about paranoia, like Craig Ferguson does in the quote that opens this chapter, but for some reason we're not as comfortable talking in a serious way about mental illness. Paranoia is often a component of mental illness. The best way I can describe it is when a person's thoughts get hijacked by extreme anxiety or fear. Normal anxiety tells you the bee flying around your head might sting you; paranoia tells you the bees are drones sent by the government to spy on you. Paranoia is a common aspect of schizophrenia, a debilitating mental illness. And marijuana can often induce a state of paranoia in users. So when research shows that smoking marijuana, particularly as a teenager, increases your risk of mental illness, this is one way they arrive at that conclusion.

Scientists at Washington University School of Medicine in St. Louis found an increased risk of suicidal thoughts in people who started smoking pot before the age of seventeen[12]. What makes the study so compelling is that they looked at identical twins, where one of the twins smoked pot and the other didn't. This type of research is unique because it compares individuals raised in a similar environment with similar genes but finds different outcomes. In the study, 277 identical-twin pairs were asked questions about their mental health and their drug use. It turned out that if you were the twin who started smoking pot, your risk of suicidal thoughts and suicide attempts was two to three times higher than that of your twin. This doesn't mean pot causes suicide, but it may mean that if you're depressed, pot may increase your downward spiral.

It may be the case that with a person who has a personal or family history of paranoia, depression, and/or suicide, using marijuana can hasten the onset of these symptoms. One important study—a "meta-analysis" which reviewed 83 published studies—found that pot users developed mental illness sooner than non–pot users, on average about three years earlier.[13] (Interestingly, the study didn't find the same relationship for alcohol or tobacco use. But it still doesn't mean that you "should" choose alcohol and cigarettes over pot.)

In any given high school, a certain percentage of students will go on to develop mental illness at some point in their lives. And I've spoken at dozens of high schools where a student recently committed suicide. Lots of schools have drug-prevention programs and lots of schools have sports and fitness programs. These are great. However, it would also be great to hear more conversations about how these activities can help reduce students' risk of mental illness and suicide. Students need to know that avoiding marijuana—and pursuing natural highs, like the ones I talk about in this book—can keep them healthy both mentally and physically during school *and* for the rest of their lives.

Where does this leave us on the issue of marijuana legalization? As my cousin said to me, "Matt, you're busy now, but if pot becomes legal you'll be even busier." The issue isn't going away anytime soon. However, I do view the debates as an opportunity to educate people about brain research and, just as important, about the value of natural highs.

Born to Move

If the act of running just sounds like medieval torture to you, then maybe you're into something else that gets the heart going. A few popular examples include basketball, cycling, skateboarding, swimming, and yoga. However, some people find themselves shying away from physical activity because they don't like the way it feels. The sweating, panting, chest tightness, and elevated heart rate of working out could also be perceived as uncomfortable or anxiety-provoking. If you think about the symptoms of a panic attack, they do look a lot like the side effects of a good run.

My wife told me that the first time she ran a mile at age thirteen she was totally out of breath. To make matters worse, she was running with her dad who insisted that they talk. I remember having a similar experience the first time I ran with her. I instantly got annoyed with her and said, "What's wrong with you? How can you talk and run at the same time?"

This discussion begs the question—are we really meant to move? Harvard anthropologist Daniel Lieberman thinks the answer is yes. He presented his theories in the 2007 Harvard Museum of Natural History's spring lecture series titled "Evolution Matters." Hopefully you live in a town in America where evolution still matters. I've visited some towns that evolution skipped over.

Dr. Lieberman's talk focused on the fact that even though more than one million humans run marathons worldwide each year, we are not animals typically associated with being good runners. Antelopes and cheetahs are built for speed and they've got humans beat, but horses and dogs are built more for distance and are not as good as humans. Although the equines and canines will run marathon-type distances if forced to do it, neither one does it as efficiently as humans. According to Dr. Lieberman, "Humans are terrible athletes in terms of power and speed, but we're phenomenal at slow and steady. We're the tortoises of the animal kingdom."

Dr. Lieberman believes that the appearance about two million years ago of physical adaptations that make humans better runners coincided with them eating meat. That's right— long before vegans ever existed, humans were meat-seeking scavengers. It is believed that eating meat—among other things— helped us to develop tendons in our legs and feet that act like large elastic bands, storing energy and releasing it with each running stride. Our bodies also developed the ability to remain stable while running, aided by our big butt muscles and an elastic ligament in our neck to keep our head stable. Dr. Lieberman also believes that our ability to lose large amounts of heat generated while running is due to our hairlessness, our ability to sweat, and the fact that we breathe rapidly when we run.

He commented, "We can run in conditions that no other animal can run in. Most animals would develop hyperthermia— heat stroke in humans—after about ten to fifteen kilometers."

Dr. Lieberman envisions an evolutionary scenario where humans began eating meat as scavengers, which allowed them to run faster to the site of a fresh kill. Evolution likely favored better runners until weapons made running less important.

If the evolution lesson above does not convince you that humans were meant to run, then go watch an episode of *The Biggest Loser*. The contestants on the show are essentially training to be endurance athletes. The fact that they start out as the complete opposite of that only makes the show more compelling. In my opinion, *The Biggest Loser* promotes an unhealthy level of exercise. It would be more realistic to show people engaged in a physical activity they love, but have them do it an hour a day every day for a year. The weight loss results would take longer, but would be no less dramatic.

Try This: Getting Started

Bob Glover, director of the New York Road Runners Club running classes, has been using the following program since 1978 to train beginner runners. Before you start, make sure you see your doctor for a physical examination, have a quality pair of running shoes, and set aside a regularly scheduled time to run. If you can walk briskly for 20 minutes without stopping to rest or becoming excessively fatigued, you are ready to go. If you can't, work up to that level, taking as much time as you need. You can also check out a great app called C25K trainer. Their tagline is "Couch Potato to 5K Runner."

Week	Workout (in minutes)	Total Run Time (in minutes)
1	Run 1, walk 2 (repeat 7 times)	7
2	Run 2, walk 2 (repeat 5 times)	10
3	Run 3, walk 2 (repeat 4 times)	12
4	Run 5, walk 2 (repeat 3 times)	15
5	Run 6, walk 1 ½ (repeat 3 times)	18
6	Run 8, walk 1 ½ (repeat 2 times)	16
7	Run 10, walk 1 ½ (repeat 2 times)	20
8	Run 12, walk 1, run 8	20
9	Run 15, walk 1, run 5	20
10	Run 20 nonstop	20

Cleveland Surfers

This chapter could have included a lot of different activities: kayaking, hiking, skateboarding, biking, or just about anything that elevates the heart rate. It just so happens that the natural high of running is well-researched, inexpensive, and popular, which makes it perfect for this chapter. However, one of my favorite *New York Times* stories in 2006 was about surfers on Lake Erie in Cleveland. That's right, Ohio. There is a small group of dedicated individuals who surf Lake Erie when the surfing is good, which happens to only be in the winter. This practice is not as unusual as you might think. I read a similar story in the *Wall Street Journal* in 2001 about a group of winter surfers in Cape Cod, and another recently in Minnesota who surf Lake Superior. In both cases, these individuals use special wetsuits made for extreme cold water. They also surf together to watch each other for signs of hypothermia.

The benefit of surfing in the winter is all about wind, which can create waves on Lake Erie that get up to ten feet high! The waves are not the cool California ones that break slowly in long tubes. Instead the waves on Lake Erie look more like haystacks that crash quickly into icy water. This particular sport has some danger associated with it, but by all accounts is pretty safe with the right clothing and precautions. You may be asking yourself, "Why would people ever do this?" Well, my favorite quote was from Cleveland surfer Bill Weeber, who said, "Surfing Lake Erie is basically disgusting. But then I catch that wave and I forget about it, and I feel high all day."

I will admit that until I read the article about the Cleveland surfers, I never really attempted to surf—in cold or warm water. But the image of people with icicles hanging out of their noses paddling out in survival suits motivated me. It didn't motivate me to fly to Cleveland—I don't know how much money that would take—but it did motivate me to take surfing lessons during a 2008 speaking trip to San Diego.

For less than $100, I had a private lesson with a former pro surfer at the Pacific Beach Surf School (www. pacificbeachsurf-school.com). The lesson included the use of a surfboard and the tightest wetsuit ever invented. Seriously, it sucked in my gut so much I looked like a ten-year-old. My instructor was Ali, a four-foot-ten-inch South American former Billabong-sponsored surfer. She's given up the pro surfing gig to make some real money teaching pale guys from New York City how to fall gracefully off a surfboard. If you are considering surfing, I've got to say just how invaluable it was to spend the hour out in the water with Ali. She showed me tips and surfed alongside of me to make sure I got up. Falling did make up 90% of my lesson, but eventually I was able to catch a wave right and stand up! Words cannot describe the surge of adrenaline that I felt that day.

It took about a year—and three more lessons—to make surfing a regular natural high. The instructor who I credit with getting me comfortable surfing on my own was Kai Sanson of Zuma Surf & Swim (www.zumasurfandswim.com). Kai is a schoolteacher who grew up surfing in Malibu and has a wonderful laid-back teaching style. I was lucky enough to be speaking near there and he really taught me a ton about the sport. If you ever get a chance to visit Malibu, think about spending a few hours then on a board, learning from him.

As a result of my lessons with Kai, my travel around the country took on a whole new sense of adventure. A speaking trip to Los Angeles or Rhode Island became not only an opportunity to talk about natural highs, but to hit the waves and experience one too!

A vacation with friends to Maine in July became an epic trip when we arrived and realized the house we rented was one block from one of Maine's best surfing spots, Gooch's Beach. Thanks to technology, you can find out the water temperature and wave heights and even see webcams of your favorite surf spots on sites like www.surfline.com. I was once in Chicago's O'Hare airport on my laptop during a thunderstorm watching guys surf in Malibu, California!

My favorite surfing natural high came in March 2010 on a trip to San Francisco. I had the morning off prior to a parent program so I drove out to a tiny town called Bolinas. My cousin had told me the waves were good there, but what he failed to tell me was that "good" meant six- to eight-footers! When I finally got to the beach, I was so nervous I turned to this guy next to me and asked, "Do you want to go in together?" He looked at me like, "Who are you?"

His name was Ben and his beard made him look close to my

age, so I felt confident when he agreed to go out with me. It took what felt like 20 minutes to get over the breaking waves out to calmer water. When we turned our boards around, I saw beautiful cliffs, blue skies, birds, and at one point a seal popped its head up out of the water. I looked at Ben and said, "We're going to die! Don't sharks eat those?"

He told me we'd have fun and we did. Two hours later, we started paddling back to shore and I asked Ben, "What do you do for a living? How can you be out here on a Tuesday morning?" He said to me, "Oh, I'm in a band. Have you have ever heard of The Fray?" My jaw dropped. I thought to myself, "Ben, 'You Found Me.'" I managed to get out, "I love your music!"

The guy I surfed with that day was Ben Wysocki, the drummer for The Fray. When I got to shore I realized that I had just experienced not one natural high, but three natural highs. In a brief period of time I managed to experience the physical exertion of surfing, the calming effect of being at the ocean, and the thrill of meeting the drummer of one of my favorite bands. Life handed me a gift—an experience so complex and rich no drug in the world could ever replicate it. The key for me was to get out there and do it. I'd almost stopped myself three times— including waking up feeling tired and not wanting to go, halfway down the long winding road to Bolinas, and the moment I got to the water and thought, "I am *not* a real man. Only real men with beards go in that water." Thankfully that man showed up and allowed me to join him.

Pick Your Brain:
The Ocean

Surfing in the ocean is a natural high for reasons other than just the great workout. Negative ions (or anions) exist at levels ten times or higher on beaches, in forests, and at waterfalls as compared to a home or office. Bright light and negative ion exposure have been shown to produce rapid changes in mood, even improving symptoms of depression. [7, 8] For example, in a study of 180 healthy Wesleyan University men and women, three 30-minute exposures of bright light and high-density negative ions significantly reduced depression scores on mood questionnaires.[8] The authors concluded that the rapid mood changes were unlikely to be a placebo effect (i.e., caused by something other than the light or anions) because the participants had "no motivational or psychological preconceptions" about the intervention.

The mechanism of action behind the mood-enhancing effect of negative ions and bright light remains unknown. Based on previous research on mood, it would be logical to conclude that bright light and negative ions are impacting levels of the neurotransmitter serotonin in the brain. Until further research is conducted, we can just smile knowing that hiking in the forest and surfing in the ocean isn't just fun, it's good for the brain as well.

Recommendation: If you're thinking about taking a surfing lesson and you're going to be in the Los Angeles area, you've got to check out Zuma Surf and Swim Training (www.zsstraining.com). Kai Swanson is such a cool instructor—he knows a ton about surfing and is incredibly patient. It also doesn't hurt that he teaches lessons in and around the Malibu area. It's worth the price of admission just to paddle along the beautiful coast there!

Try This: What is your "running" type natural high? Do you snowboard, surf, skateboard, play tennis, basketball, or something else? If you have an exercise natural high that you enjoy, do you do it as much as you would like to? If not, consider adding something else to your repertoire. Perhaps reconsider a physical activity that you had previously dismissed as "not for you." Make a list of the positive and negative things about the activity. Then ask yourself if the reasons for not trying it could be overcome, either by wearing better, exercise-specific clothing or just developing a different perspective—like I did by starting to run in the cold weather.

Wrap-Up

The runner's high is much more than just the release of opiates from one part of the brain to the other. The experience of a natural high during a run seems to vary from feelings of everyday accomplishment and stress relief to the exhilaration of completing a marathon. The runner's high also comes from much more than just running since there are dozens of activities that can challenge your body and your mind. The key is trying out many different activities that involve exercise in order to see which one (or more) is best suited for you. If there is one thing to learn from runners it's that with time and effort, you *will* get stronger and more confident. If your natural high activity doesn't bring you a high the first time, try, try again.

Chapter 4

Eating, Cooking and Other Highs Better Than Alcohol

When you don't drink, people always ask why. "You don't drink? Why?"
This never happens with anything else.
"You don't use mayonnaise? Why? Are you addicted to mayonnaise?
"Is it OK if I use mayonnaise?"
—Jim Gaffigan

Growing up as an Italian-American in New Jersey, I had many opportunities to enjoy great food. Whether it was a slice of Papa Tony's pizza in Cedar Grove, a Jersey Mike's Italian sub in Point Pleasant, or my grandma's rigatoni with meatballs in Collingswood, I ate well. Thanks to my mother, I always ate pretty healthy, too. She wasn't into buying sugary cereal or fast food, so I developed good habits. The only problem was that I didn't appreciate how great I had it in terms of the quality of the food I ate at home. It wasn't until I went away to college in Pennsylvania that I realized the rest of the world does not eat like my family. I was truly miserable. It was the Dark Ages of food for me.

Eating raises blood sugar levels and releases the feel-good chemical dopamine in the brain. When dopamine is released, mood elevation typically occurs. Eating is obviously vital for all of us, so the fact that the brain makes it pleasurable ensures that we will want to eat again. When I eat something that tastes good, it's almost like my brain feels happy—a natural high. I know it because my eyes begin to tear up, I go on and on about how great the food is, and sometimes I even take pictures of the food. Some of my friends think it's a little weird, but when they need a restaurant recommendation, they treat me like Urbanspoon.

I really didn't begin to appreciate the full range of good food out there until I began cooking. I read recently that one of the best ways to get a child to eat different foods is to invite him or her into the kitchen so that they can become part of the cooking process. I had to wait until I was in college to get struck by the cooking bug. The cafeteria at my school was a step above awful. The only thing it had going for it was that it was "all you can eat." To me the food was so horrible they should have put up a sign that read, "All you should eat," with a picture showing tiny portions on a plate.

I finally got fed up (pun intended) in my junior year when it became depressing for me to go the cafeteria. I begged my mother to send me the money that she would've given to the food services people for my meal plan. With that money, I began to buy and cook my own food. That semester I ate like a king, not just because I could choose what I wanted, but also because my food was fresh from the produce stand. Guys would stop by my room and ask me how they could get on my meal plan. The only downside was that during the week I started eating alone more often, because everybody else was still suffering through the cafeteria. I quickly learned that a big part of the eating natural high is sharing it with good friends and family.

When I was in graduate school I finally had an apartment— and more importantly a kitchen—of my own. Each day I would work hard in the biology lab (often getting frustrated when my experiments weren't working) and each night I returned home to watch Molto Mario on the Food Network make dinner. It was a sad existence until it dawned on me that I should start to make some of the dishes I was seeing on television.

The only problem was that I was broke. Then one night I watched Mario make gnocchi with pesto. Gnocchi is potato pasta, which combines two things I love, potatoes and pasta. When I realized that all it took to make the pasta was two potatoes, eggs, and flour, I was blown away. "Even I can do that!" I thought.

Several failed attempts later, I made some pretty good-looking gnocchi. What about the sauce? Well, I cheated at first and just bought some pesto sauce. When I tossed the whole thing together I almost fell off my borrowed couch. I was eating a gourmet meal that would cost me over $20 in a restaurant. Soon my eyes welled up and I was taking pictures like a fool.

In graduate school, I was fortunate to live near my Grandma Rose's house. Every weekend, I would go over for ziti and meatballs. Those meatballs were a genuine natural high. They were made with veal, pork, and beef and simmered slowly in tomato sauce. They were also cooked with love. When they were done, she would top them with Pecorino Romano cheese that created a smell and flavor so amazing my eyes got teary. I used to think I could learn to cook those meatballs, and eventually I did—but mine never tasted quite the same. I think the missing ingredient will always be eating with Grandma at her kitchen table. She asked me once why I wasn't out at some bar like other young people my age and I responded, "There's no bar in the world teaching how to make these meatballs."

Better Eating Means a Better Mood

Not to brag, but in January of 2007 I spent a week speaking in the rural Midwest. While at the local Walmart, I told the checkout clerk that I was in the area for the week and she said, "You're stuck here all week? I'm so sorry!" I looked at her and said, *"You're* sorry? You *live* here." Honestly, it was a decent enough place, but being away from home for a week in the dead of winter makes many places seem dull. On my way back to the hotel, I remember feeling really down and just endlessly scanning the radio stations seeking entertainment. As I pulled into the parking lot, I settled on a station where I heard a caller telling a story about the biggest surprise of her life. This is basically what she said:

"I was dog-sitting for my friends who had this really big, really old dog. On the second night, the dog fell asleep and never woke up! I was panicked, so I called the vet. He calmed me by saying, 'Don't worry. He was old, just bring him over tomorrow.' Weighing as much as the dog, I had no idea how to get it to the vet. So I looked around their house and found a large suitcase..."

At this point of the story, I was about to leave my car. It wasn't that funny, but it sounded interesting and hey, I was stuck in the middle of nowhere.

"...Once I got the dog in the suitcase I realized that I didn't have access

to a car nor would a cab be an option. There was no way I was going to have a cab driver catch me with this thing. So I set off for the subway. The wheels on the suitcase made the trip very easy. I took the escalator down to my train, got off at the stop, and was devastated to learn that the escalator was out! I began pulling the suitcase up the stairs and must have looked ridiculous, because a man offered his help. He looked a little sketchy, but I needed the help. As he pulled the suitcase up the stair, he asked, 'What's in this thing?' I told him it was computer equipment and as he reached the top of the stairs, I reached for my wallet to give him a tip. Just then he turned and sprinted down the street with the suitcase!"

At that point, I just busted out laughing because I didn't see it coming. The story made me laugh because it evoked such powerful images. I could picture the look of horror on the faces of her friends when she explained that their dog was not only dead, but stolen! At the same time, I imagined the stunned look on the robber's face when he opened the suitcase! I know it's completely callous of me to laugh when we're talking about a dead dog. I love dogs, but at that moment, it was just a shockingly funny story. The reason I'm retelling the story is because of what happened next.

The laughter from the radio story lifted my spirits momentarily, but it was precisely those next few moments when I was thinking about dinner. The previous few nights I had purchased some food and eaten back in my sad hotel room. But after that laugh, I was so motivated by the good feelings that I decided to treat myself to a decent meal. A decent meal there meant an hour's drive to a P.F. Chang's, but it was totally worth it. The entire evening boosted my mood. I was calling old friends from the car, I was chatting it up with the wait staff at the restaurant. It all began with the natural high of laughter, and ended with the natural high of eating great food. Well, good food at least—it *was* a P.F. Chang's.

Inspirational Pizza

I ate a pizza once that was so good it made me cry. There is nothing creepier than a grown man eating and weeping.
—Matt Bellace

Try This: Your Eating Bucket List

For me, one of the best things about living in New York City is access to great pizza. When it's done right (i.e., fresh mozzarella, San Marzano tomatoes, and crispy crust) it's the perfect food. Of course, if you live in the Southeast the perfect food might be an amazing barbecue or fried seafood plate, in the Southwest it could be Tex-Mex, and on the West Coast, well, just about everything tastes great to me out there.

I think it's fun to create your top five favorite places to eat and then explore new places as you travel around. Below are my own top five favorite pizza places in the country. I hope you'll consider visiting a few of these wonderful places and think of me taking pictures and crying. How about *your* list? If you're inspired by my top five, go ahead and write down your top five all-time places to eat.

Kesté, 271 Bleecker Street, New York, New York

This Greenwich Village pizza spot is arguably the best pizza in New York City. The owner trained in Naples, Italy, and is so obsessed with making pizza the right way he flew in an expert pizza-oven builder from Italy to make the oven. This Neapolitan pizza may cost a little more, but it's completely worth it. Also, if the tiny place is packed and you have to wait to get in, check out the famous Murray's Cheese down the block.

Varasano's Pizzeria, 2171 Peachtree Road, Atlanta, Georgia

When I used to think about food in Atlanta, I would imagine peaches and some type of tree nut—not great pizza. However, this image was shattered the second I took a look at the Margherita pizza at Varasano's in the Buckhead section of the city. A flight delay out of New York put me in around 9 PM and extreme hunger had me assuming the food would stink. I don't know why my mind does that when I'm hungry—it's like I become more of a food snob when I'm starving. The atmosphere was hip and the pizzas came out from the oven blistering hot with the perfect blend of cheese and tomatoes. It's no surprise that the owner, Jeff Varasano, is a pizza authority who grew up in New York City.

Piece Pizza, 1927 West North Avenue, Chicago, Illinois

A college buddy of mine, Steve Gerrity, wrote me about this

thin-crust place in Chicago, the home of the deep dish. I love Chicago deep dish, but I have yet to bite into a deep dish pie and get that feeling of perfection that I do with that first taste of thin crust. I almost get the sense that Chicago deep dish is more for tourists. Although located in Chicago, Piece Pizza is actually an almost exact replication of the New Haven, Connecticut, style pizza made famous by places like Sally's and Pepe's on Wooster Street. The difference is that Piece is totally laid-back and easier to get into. The best advice Steve gave me, though, was to follow a Piece pie with a walk around the corner for the best hot chocolate in Chicago at a place called Hot Chocolate. The combination of these two killer spots is definitely a natural high.

2Amys Pizza, 3715 Macomb Street NW, Washington, DC
I was recently speaking at the Sidwell Friends School in D.C. The school is probably best known for two things—the Obama girls and being down the block from 2Amys. The style of pizza at 2Amys is thin-crust Neapolitan, which means it is only cooked in a wood-burning oven. It felt like I was back in Italy enjoying a lunchtime meal. My favorite is the Margherita pizza—simply tomato, buffalo mozzarella, and basil. I also loved the laid-back atmosphere and great appetizers.

Motorino, 349 East 12th Street, New York, New York
Owner Mathieu Palombino bought the storefront and wood-burning oven of the famous Una Pizza Napoletana after it suddenly closed in 2009. My wife and I had a date night there recently and I was skeptical it could live up to the reputation of its puritanical predecessor. However, after sampling the bread and heavenly Margherita pizza I became a believer. Every pie uses buffalo mozzarella and imported San Marzano tomatoes. Afterwards, we were lucky to meet Mathieu. His passion for creating great pizza was evident as he explained his process of experimenting with 25 different doughs during the past year. If you eat there, do yourself a favor and have dessert around the corner at the Momofuku Milk Bar. I recommend the Cereal Milk soft-serve ice cream.

Honorable Mentions: Sally's Apizza (New Haven, Connecticut), Pizzeria Bianco (Phoenix, Arizona), Star Tavern (Orange, New Jersey), A16 (San Francisco, California).

Honorable Mentions: Pizzeria Mozza (various locations), Una Pizza Napoletana (San Francisco, California)

Pick Your Brain:
Eating and the Brain

In recent years, obesity researchers have been exploring the neurological pathways involved in eating and overeating. The mesolimbic brain pathway is a complex neural network that regulates many emotional and motivational processes involved in reward. Eating is an inherently rewarding process. The process of eating often begins with feelings of hunger, which at times can be uncomfortable. The hungrier you get, the more you want to eat.

Once you've eaten, the discomfort decreases while feelings of satiation and pleasure increase. Dopamine is the neurochemical that's believed to be involved in the good feelings as well as the "wanting" part of eating. The "liking" part of eating is believed to be mediated by different neurochemicals known as opiates.[1] A recent study showed that increasing opiates in the brain of an animal that's already eaten can actually cause it to eat more than an animal that is just food-deprived.[2]

Taking in certain nutrients, such as fats and sugars, can produce significant effects on the brain and behavior. It's fascinating to me that the same neural pathway is used when someone eats sugars and fats as when someone takes addictive drugs. When fats and sugars are consumed in excess, this releases a greater amount of dopamine than it typically would from a balanced meal, similar to the process involved when someone abuses cocaine or amphetamines.[3]

Laboratory studies have shown that rats will binge when offered sugar and fat separately, but that the combination of sweet and fat together produces the most pronounced binges. For example, rats will consume almost 60% of their daily calorie intake within a two-hour binge when given ample access to a combination of sweets and fats.[4] In a way, the rat experiment might explain the long lines at Cold Stone Creamery. It does not, however, explain my father's need to comment on it. We'd need a research project on just him to figure that out.

I've got to admit that these results are consistent with my

personal experience. I have finished big meals—I mean, huge meals where I am completely full—and somehow reading about food can make me want more. It's like I'm thinking, "You know, I'm disgustingly bloated and full right now, but reading this word 'tiramisu' makes me want to eat more." If reading this chapter causes you to want to eat despite being full, I apologize. Enjoy the meal.

Learning How to Eat: Slow Food

During a trip to Italy in 2007, my wife and I had quite an eating adventure. We were staying in the Tuscany region and each day we would travel to these small hill towns, walk around, and eat the most incredible food you could imagine. I ate a Tuscan bread soup called ribollita that gave me the symptoms of an eating natural high—watering eyes, big smiles, and wild statements like "This is the best soup on earth!" I ordered ribollita every time I saw it on a menu in Tuscany and was never disappointed.

Inevitably, at some point after every meal there we'd be, walking around town, and come across a gathering of people sitting outside at tables with a sign that read "Slow Food Movement." Italians are not exactly known for eating quickly, so that concept seemed kind of funny to us. Perhaps they thought three-hour dinners were not long enough.

It turns out that the Slow Food movement had finally hit its tipping point and was receiving international attention. Its simple concept: everyone has a fundamental right to eat good, clean food. The movement was founded upon the strong connections between the plate and our planet. Its proponents believe that eating well should not harm the environment, animal welfare, or our health. They also believe that food producers should receive fair compensation for their work.

The movement actually began in Italy, back in 1986. The founding father of the Slow Food movement, Italian Carlo Petrini, recognized that the industrialization of food was actually making our food taste worse and also reducing the variety of food available in supermarkets. He wanted to reach out to consumers and demonstrate to them that they have choices above and beyond fast food and processed supermarket items.

Petrini rallied his friends and his community, and began to speak out at every available opportunity about the effects of a fast-food culture. His main priority was to support and protect small growers and artisanal producers, which basically means he was all about small-scale food production—not mass-produced food. The greater goal was to protect the environment and promote diversity in the foods we consume. It's hard to find diversity in mass-produced foods because the system is set up to churn out a few items many times.

Today, the organization that Petrini and his colleagues founded is active in over 100 countries and has a worldwide membership of over 80,000 people.

An understanding of the Slow Food movement is vital to a chapter on healthy eating natural highs. The culture of fast food and prepackaged everything in supermarkets has disconnected people from the origins of their food. For example, when you go to a fast-food place and order some nugget of chicken, deep fried and dipped in high-sugar sauce, you're completely removed from any part of the food processing. You don't see the chicken ahead of time. You barely even see it while you are eating it. Unless you bite the nugget in half and make a point to look at it before you dip, how do you know if it's white or green? Presumably, the chicken nugget is safe to eat. But is it good to eat?

Earlier in this chapter I talked about the connection between foods high in fat and sugar and binge eating. Fast food provides us with a perfect example of an unhealthy natural high. It's loaded with sugar and fat, which is carefully engineered in the laboratory to taste great and leave you wanting more. But eating is a natural high that should ideally be a healthy natural high. The only way to achieve this is to eat a balanced diet that consists of more natural foods. And natural foods tend not to be processed into high-fat, high-sugar nuggets.

When I was a kid, if you gave me a choice I would have eaten Easy Cheese and anything with ketchup. For me, basically what it came down to was that there were two food groups: ketchup, and all things that you ate with ketchup. Thankfully, my mother exposed me to other foods. I might not have wanted them right away, but I think she hoped one day I'd appreciate healthier food.

You may not love Italian food—perhaps you prefer Thai, Mexican, Indian, or Southwestern cooking. It really doesn't matter what type of cuisine you like, the Slow Food movement is more about choosing locally grown meats and produce that represent the true flavors of food. In fact, if you travel to the country of origin of your favorite foods you'll find that the best restaurants tend to serve foods made from the freshest, most local ingredients.

The truth is if everyone decided to eat only fresh, natural foods, we probably wouldn't have an obesity problem because it's too expensive! You can't overeat when you can't afford it. Buying healthy food can leave your wallet looking pretty unhealthy. But imagine the changes in our food supply if every family suddenly chose to buy one more meal a week at a farmer's market rather than a fast-food spot. When you vote with your wallet like that, things start to change. If we think long term, there would be fewer health costs years from now if people spent more on better food today.

One of the best areas of the country to experience the Slow Food movement is in California. In fact, the state looks so much like Italy that sometimes I mess it up in my brain and refer to our trips to California as our trips to Italy! I feel like in California, you can walk into almost any food establishment and get fresher, less processed food than you can anywhere else in the country.

One of the reasons that California has developed into the Slow Food capital of the United States is the influence of Alice Waters. If Carlo Patrini is the father of the Slow Food movement, then Alice Waters is the mother. Thirty-seven years ago she started a restaurant in Berkeley, California, called Chez Panisse. But it wasn't just the delicious cooking that made her famous—it was the ingredients. She was one of the first to serve antibiotic- and hormone-free meats and insisted on fresh, organic, locally grown fruits and vegetables.

The good news for many people is that the organic movement has gotten stronger in our country. Even Walmart now sells organic produce! If you look, I'm sure you can find locally grown products near you. For example, not too far from where I live are the Berkshire Mountains of Western Massachusetts, where you can find ample locally grown pork and cheese products. If you're one of the millions of people who commute to the Jersey Shore or the Hamptons in the summer, there are dozens of local farmers who sell their locally grown fruits and vegetables along the side of the road. In the state of Washington, you'll find the freshest salmon and apples anywhere. Wisconsin's amazing cheese or Florida's oranges are well known, but how about California's avocadoes or Maryland's crabs? I feel like every state has some great food to offer if you look.

Try This: Do you like to eat out? Pick up a Zagat Guide or check out Menupages.com and note the restaurants that serve your favorite cuisine. Select two or three with the highest food ratings that are still in your price range, and try them out. Chances are you'll find that the food is fresher and better-tasting than the fast-food versions. For more information about the Slow Food movement, check out www.slowfood.com. To find the nearest farmer's market near you, visit www.localharvest.org/.

Learning How to Eat: Your Own Cooking

Anyone who travels for a living knows that sometimes healthy food is hard to find. I remember on this one trip, there was literally only one restaurant in town and it was attached to a gas station. Their most popular item was fried cheese curds, which are chunks of uncooked cheddar dipped in batter and fried. They were delicious, but it's probably one of those "once a year" treats, not an everyday item, unless you like getting angioplasty procedures to clean out your arteries. The funniest part for me was when the waitress handed me a bottle and said, "You can't have these without ranch dressing."

I lived in a poor food town for almost six years and when I couldn't travel, I made the good stuff at home. In this age of the internet, amazing eats are just a few YouTube clicks away. One great way to learn how to cook is by watching authentic cooking shows. I'm talking about the Iron Chef types who can really cook. For the Italian food fan, that means Lidia Bastianich of the PBS show *Lidia's Italy* or Mario Batalli of Fine Living Network's *Molto Mario*. There are also a slew of great demos on YouTube of cooks making dishes that will give you the eating natural high.

Once you have the ingredients you need and a kitchen in which to cook them, my advice is to start simple. Pick out one dish that you think would be cool to make at home, like pizza or soup. Focus all of your energy on one dish and keep trying it until you perfect it. It's important to remember that the ingredients are everything for great dishes. If you can't find a particular ingredient in your local supermarket, you may need to try a specialty shop or mail order. I wouldn't start with something that requires expensive ingredients. You don't want to be paying back a failed white truffle dish forever.

If you have a real interest in cooking, maybe you can find a cooking class that'll teach you the basics. Cooking always got a bad rap in middle school among my friends. They said it was "gay." That was their favorite word for everything. I always found it ironic that what they thought was unmasculine got me more dates in my twenties than all the kickball home runs I ever made in gym class. In my opinion, there are few things more intimate than breaking bread with friends or a romantic interest. There's just something about giving the gift of good food that feels great.

Try This:

At this point, you've read about at two least meals that gave me a natural high. So why not take the next step and make these recipes at home? You'll have fun, I promise! And hey—take a picture of the dish and share it with me via Instagram or Twitter, OK?

Grandma's Meatballs

Old-school Italian grandmas almost never wrote down their recipes. My grandma was no exception, so I shadowed her in the kitchen a bunch of times as she made her famous meatballs. The only downside to making this recipe is that it may ruin your ability to enjoy other people's versions because—trust me—they won't be nearly as good.

Ingredients:

1 slice good-quality white bread

1/3 cup milk

½ pound *each* ground beef, ground pork, ground veal

1 egg, lightly beaten

1 tablespoon yellow onion, chopped fine

1 tablespoon olive oil

1 28-ounce can Italian plum tomatoes (I like the San Marzano brand), crushed by hand

½ cup Parmigiano-reggiano cheese, freshly grated

1 tablespoon fresh parsley, chopped; *or* dried parsley

1 teaspoon salt

Black pepper (preferably freshly ground), to taste

Enough vegetable oil *or* olive oil to fill the bottom of a large sauté pan

Freshly grated Pecorino Romano cheese for the table

1. Trim away the bread's crust. Put the milk and the bread in a bowl and let it sit for 10 minutes. When the bread has soaked up the milk, mash it up with a fork.
2. Into a bowl put the ground meats, onion, parsley, egg, olive oil, Parmigiano-Reggiano cheese, the milk- mashed bread, and several grindings of black pepper. Gently knead the mixture with your hands, trying not to squeeze it too hard. When all the ingredients are evenly combined, gently shape the mixture into balls about 1 inch in diameter. My grandmother used to make them more like 2 inches in diameter, but it's up to you.
3. Here's the big step that will ensure great meatballs. Choose a sauté pan that can hold all of the meatballs in a single layer. If you need to do two or three batches, that's fine too. Just don't try to crowd or stack them.
4. Pour oil into the large pan and turn heat to medium high. When the oil is hot, slip in the meatballs using a spatula to avoid splashing the hot oil. Brown the meatballs on all sides (this can be a little tricky, so don't worry when at least one side ends up odd-shaped).
5. Remove the pan from the heat and tip it to remove as much of the oil and fat as possible with a spoon. Be careful not to burn yourself!
6. Return the pan to the burner over medium heat; add crushed tomatoes with their juice, and a pinch of salt. Make sure to turn the meatballs a few times to coat them in the sauce.
7. Cover the pan and lower the heat to let them simmer for about 20 to 25 minutes.

My grandma used to boil rigatoni pasta and serve the meatballs and sauce over the rigatoni with grated Pecorino Romano cheese on top. If you're like me, the moment the first bite touches your mouth will be a true natural high. Enjoy!

Gnocchi with Pesto

I've read that the Italian town of Veneto is where gnocchi were first made, but, to my dismay, I've never been there. I don't remember the first time I ate gnocchi, but the first time I *made* gnocchi will live in my memory forever. I ended up with a meal that blended so many of my favorite flavors, including warm potato, cheese, and basil. I was living in a second-floor bland-looking apartment in Lewisburg, Pennsylvania, with a borrowed couch and a mattress on the floor. I was a second-year graduate student and as I continued to work on my thesis, every day felt like an uphill climb. My reward for struggling to get my experiments to work in the biology lab? Coming home to cook in the rundown kitchen. The moment I finished making gnocchi, I felt like I was at a gourmet restaurant in a cool city somewhere. I hope that when you finish this dish, you'll feel the same way.

I'm a total nut for pesto sauce and I really enjoy making it, so I've included my recipe below. If you're not feeling quite so adventurous, try a good-quality store-bought pesto sauce. And if you don't like pesto, I've added a quickie recipe for brown butter and sage sauce, which is also amazing. Of course, feel free to use any other sauce that you like.

One piece of advice when you go shopping: choose the potatoes wisely! The typical "boiling" potato, which is almost round, is the one you want—not the more elongated "baking" potato. (If in doubt, ask somebody working in the produce section.)

Gnocchi ingredients:

1 ½ pounds "boiling" potatoes
1 ½ cups unbleached all-purpose flour

1. Heat a large pot of water to a boil. Put the potatoes in with their skins. Let them boil for at least 12 minutes, then test them by puncturing a few with a fork. If the fork goes in smoothly, they're all done. Drain the potatoes, let them sit for 5 to10 minutes, and then pull off their skins while warm (not hot) and mash them with a strong fork, a ricer, or a food processor. Place in a large bowl.
2. Add most of the flour to the mashed-up potatoes and knead them into a smooth mixture. Stop when the mixture becomes soft and smooth, but is still sticky.

3. Dust the surface of your counter with flour. Divide the potato and flour mixture into 2 balls, and then roll them out in 1-inch-thick rods.
4. Cut the rods into pieces about ¾ inch long. Make sure you dust your hands as you go to keep them from getting sticky.
5. If you like, finish the shape of the gnocchi by taking a dinner fork and rolling each piece you've cut with the back of the fork. This will create slight indentations in the gnocchi and allow the sauce to stick to it that much better. If you don't have the time, don't worry—I've seen some restaurants serve them without this little flourish and they still taste amazing!
6. Place the gnocchi in a flour-dusted pan and let them sit until you're ready to boil them.
7. Boil 4 quarts of water and add two or three teaspoons of salt to the water. This is important because you won't salt the pasta when it's done. Trust me, this makes a difference in how the pasta tastes, but if you're skeptical, do an experiment yourself to test it!
8. Once the water is simmering, put in the gnocchi two at a time. They'll float to the surface in about a minute or so. Scoop them out, ideally with a slotted spoon, into a bowl with the pesto sauce on the bottom. You don't need to warm the sauce beforehand, because the heat from the gnocchi will take care of it. Gently mix the gnocchi and pesto together until you can see a nice coating on the pasta.
9. Enjoy with your favorite vegetable and some Pellegrino water for good measure and it'll feel like you're living in Veneto, Italy.

Pesto ingredients:
This calls for a food processor or mini food chopper. You could do it by hand, but you'll need a mortar and pestle from the Dark Ages.

2 cups fresh basil leaves, tightly packed

1 garlic clove, chopped fine

½ cup extra-virgin olive oil

A pinch of salt

3 tablespoons pine nuts, walnuts, *or* pistachios (optional)

For addition at the end:
½ cup Parmigiano-Reggiano cheese, freshly grated
2 tablespoons Pecorino Romano cheese, freshly grated

1. Briefly soak and wash the basil in cold water. Gently and thoroughly pat it dry, using paper towels.
2. Put the basil, olive oil, nuts (if using), garlic, and salt in the processor and run it on low until the mixture has a creamy consistency.
3. Transfer the mixture into a bowl and mix in the two grated cheeses using a spatula or spoon. When the cheese has evenly distributed, set aside until your pasta is ready.

Not into pesto? Another great sauce for gnocchi is brown butter and sage. You just take a stick of unsalted butter (1/2 cup), cut it into slices about an inch thick, then place the slices in a pan large enough to hold your pasta later. Heat on low heat until they're melted and starting to brown a bit. Then add four or five little stalks of sage, washed and chopped fine and then cook for a minute or so. Toss the cooked gnocchi in the pan with the butter and sage and enjoy!

The Pellegrino Revolution

I am Italian-American and I do not drink wine, which can be shocking to my family. My uncle once said, "You don't drink wine? How do you eat your food?" I was thinking, "Um . . . I chew it." I've spent time in vineyards, tasted Chiantis and Pinot Grigios, and learned about the process of producing wines, but the taste of wine does nothing for me. I respect the rights of any adult to enjoy wine or any alcohol in moderation, but it is not for me. As a high school student I didn't drink because I didn't want to get into trouble. In college I was a social activist making a point. Now, despite knowing that I can drink, I decide not to because of the taste.

In people over age 21, "moderate drinking" is defined as one or two drinks per day. Consuming more than this increases your risk of developing many types of cancers and dementia (e.g., Alzheimer's).[5,6] My maternal grandmother suffered from

Alzheimer's dementia and I know it is not something I want more of in my life.

Interestingly, many people drink to excess during what could simply be natural high events, like meals, comedy shows, or sporting events. In fact, there are times when the chemical high overwhelms the natural high and people's behavior changes for the worse. I remember one particular comedy show when a woman—who appeared to be very intoxicated—thought that one of my jokes was her personal invitation to join me on stage. She actually made her way onto the stage and grabbed for the microphone just before her horrified boyfriend pulled her away. It was such a bizarre moment that as they left the club during my set, I called out, "Don't leave, you're the funniest thing that will happen here all night!"

There are many nonalcoholic drinks that I find go well with a great meal. Sparkling water, like Pellegrino, is one of my favorites. If that's not your thing, there are all kinds of specialty iced teas, lemonades, and vitamin drinks that not only taste great, but some are good for you. True, a lot of them have tons of sugar and artificial flavors, but drinks like Honest Tea tastes great with minimal sugar. Of course, we shouldn't forget fresh cold water. So many people convince themselves that they hate water, but try a nice sweaty workout in the summer and cold water might be the first thing on your mind.

In recent years, there's been a big movement in schools away from offering sodas and other sugary drinks in an effort to combat obesity. I think it's great for schools to model healthier habits.

Try This: Make an effort to try healthier beverage options. For example, if you consume three cans of soda per day, try drinking only one with dinner. If you live on beverages like diet soda, perhaps try something more natural like hot or iced tea with honey. If you have doubts that you'll enjoy it, do an experiment. Give it two weeks and see if you experience changes in mood or energy levels. Dehydration from caffeinated sugary drinks like Red Bull and Mountain Dew are believed to contribute to fatigue and daytime sleepiness. You may have to give up the Coke or Pepsi, but you may also give up the fighting to stay awake in the afternoon.

Wrap-Up

Eating when you're hungry or drinking when you're thirsty simply feels good. For myself, I look forward to the summer because I love that sensation of sweating, getting really thirsty, and then quenching that thirst with a tall, cold glass of water. The natural high of eating comes from the increase in blood sugar in the body and the release of dopamine in the reward centers of the brain. Experiencing eating natural highs, in my opinion, is also about being open-minded to trying new foods, drinks, and cooking techniques. And for me, good food is always better when shared with good friends.

Chapter 5

Helping, Listening and Other Highs Better Than Being Selfish

You ever find yourself being lazy for no reason at all?
Like you pick up your mail and realize you have a letter for
a neighbor—and you say to yourself, "Hmmm, they're never getting this.
Takes too much energy to go outside."
—Jim Gaffigan

What motivates the motivator? There are some days when I get up and feel like I would rather do nothing. There are days that I don't feel like being funny and don't want to perform. These feelings usually change the instant I see a crowd waiting for me. But the travel is hard on the spirit. I can only take so many days in a row of waking up in a Hampton Inn and finding mystery hair in the shower before I start to lose it. I remember missing home so much once that I started to tear up during the Michael Buble song "I Wanna Go Home." In my defense, that song could probably break Clint Eastwood.

The things that motivate me tend to be meeting individuals who've overcome circumstances far more difficult than mine. During my freshman year at Bucknell I met Steven Starkey, a young man so inspirational that just seeing him would change my mood for the rest of the day. Steven didn't look like the other students at Bucknell. He was a heavyset young man who wore a long beard and often dressed in sweats and a t-shirt. But he didn't seem fazed one bit that his appearance wasn't fashionable.

Steven lived on the same hall as some of my friends and it

was easy to get to know him because all you needed to say was "Hello." A conversation with Steven usually ended the same way every time—me walking away, him continuing to talk, and me waving goodbye so as not to hurt his feelings. I soon learned that he'd been diagnosed with a brain tumor during his junior year in high school. It was inoperable and would one day take his life.

He knew this and despite all of it was at college anyway. The doctors gave him chemotherapy and tried to shrink the tumor, but they couldn't remove it. It eventually grew and pushed against the speech and motor areas of his brain, impairing his functioning. When Steven walked, he moved very slowly, dragging one leg behind him. When he talked, he slurred his speech and you had to take time to understand him. Everything about Steven was in slow motion on a campus that moved very fast.

I was told that the medications he took made him tired and it was difficult for him to stay awake at night to study. The medication also left him feeling exhausted every morning and his roommate told me just how impossible it was getting him up for class. By all accounts, Steven had a life that was far too hard for someone so young.

What inspired me about Steven was that, despite his illness, he was still at college. At the age of eighteen, there were about a dozen things I would have rather been doing than going to college. Not Steven. He was studying to become a teacher and he was an active member of a service fraternity and a religious group on campus. His life was literally about helping others or preparing to help others. He was doing all of these things while dealing with the insensitive reactions of those who didn't know his story. I can recall seeing someone complain about being stuck behind Steven on their way up a flight of stairs because she was late to class. I remember seeing a student knock into him with a book bag and not even apologize. He dealt with this day after day.

I was lucky enough to know Steven and every time I would see him in the hall or on the quad, his presence was motivating to me. My problems would fade away because I realized that Steven's reality was far tougher than mine and his problems much scarier.

The night before graduation, the class of 1996 and their families filled the Weis Performing Arts Center for an achievement awards ceremony. I was never big on awards, but since I was getting one I thought I would show up. It actually felt great to be recognized for my hard work as a social activist on campus. The final award that night was presented to the student who "earned his degree while overcoming tremendous obstacles."

When they announced Steven Starkey, there was the initial round of cordial applause, but no sign of Steven. Several seconds passed and I could see him starting to make his way slowly to the stage. As he limped and lumbered his way down the aisle the applause began to build. It erupted into a standing ovation. I imagined that the guilt of so many students who had dismissed Steven for four years was now coming to the surface. He accepted his award to the loudest applause of the night. I was choking up. And I was totally bummed because he didn't get to make a speech! It would have been so cool to see Steven take the mike and talk until we all left the building.

Steven Starkey died in 1998. We had lost touch after college, but I understand from friends that after graduation he was working on finishing his teaching certification. The image of Steven is still fresh in my mind. He represented more than just hard work and persistence. Steven represented the importance of helping others. Steven may not have always had a happy life, but because he spent his time on this earth serving others I do believe he had a good life.

His goodness comes back to me when I lose perspective on my problems. Sometimes when I wake up feeling not funny or lazy, I think of Steven. I remember what he stood for and even if I am lumbering, I get out of bed and try my best to help other people.

Big Tip Night

Here's a great example of a natural high that I learned from my friends at T.I.G.S. It's "big tip night." (I learned the hard way that you've got to say that one slowly in front of an audience.) The idea was simple. We gathered together a bunch of friends—ten or so—and decided to go out for ice cream. In New Jersey we have these restaurants called Friendly's, which serve great ice-cream sundaes. We arrived about 20 minutes before they closed, knowing that seeing a huge group of teenagers at that time would ruin any wait staff's night.

But before we went in, everyone chipped in an extra $5 to $10 for the tip. By the time we were done we had about $75 on what would be a $50 bill. I can't remember ever having more fun eating ice cream, because of course, we were loud and laughing like crazy knowing what was about to happen. Once we finally finished, we put the money in a card and my friend filled it out with the greeting "We think the best way to make the world a better place is to do good things for people." Then we all signed the card and made a quick exit. Once outside we did our best not to appear conspicuous as we peeked inside and watched the reaction of our waitress. The smile on her face as she opened that card could have filled the room.

Try This: Try your own version of "big tip night." If you can, gather together a bunch of friends who also like helping others. Write me at matt@mattbellace.com and let me know how it went.

Running for Someone

Knowing I'm a dad with two little kids, people often ask me, "Is it hard to be on the road, away from your family?"
I respond, "No, it's fantastic!"
—Matt Bellace

My answer in the quote above is usually true for the first night. After a good meal and a full night's sleep, though, I start missing my family. However, I'll admit that recently it was a trip that was so much fun I had to downplay it when I called home. There are just some things that should go unsaid to keep a marriage and a family going.

I spent an entire week in Orange County, California. I would speak at schools in the morning, surf in the afternoon, and then speak at a parent program at night followed by a late dinner at one of several great pizza places. The time difference was part of the reason I felt so energized. My eyes would open at 6 AM and I'd be wide awake, so I'd head to the hotel gym. I basically got to work out, eat great food, and speak about natural highs to thousands of students and parents all in one week.

The highlight of the entire trip occurred one afternoon while

I was surfing near the pier in Newport Beach. There was a surf lesson going on about 50 yards away with a half-dozen ten-year-olds and an instructor. It was fun listening to the encouragement they gave each other as they attempted to catch the waves. The instructor had an oversized board and one of the students was on it with him. Every few minutes the instructor caught a wave and the two of them stood up together. At that point, all the other students erupted in cheers and they were joined by people watching from the pier. They caught a few more waves together and each time the crowd went nuts.

When the lesson ended, I watched the students paddle in and drag their boards onto the beach. When the instructor and his student on the board went in, they caught one more wave and again the crowd cheered wildly. It was on their way up the beach when I noticed the instructor was helping the young man walk in the sand. It appeared he had some physical condition, like cerebral palsy, preventing him from walking on his own. I couldn't believe it. I had no idea the boy had any disability while he was out in the water.

I paddled back in and found the instructor as he was packing up his van. I told him how uplifting it was to watch him ride waves with the boy and then listen to the crowd cheer for him. The instructor was grinning from ear to ear as he told me, "His walking has improved since he started the lessons." To me, that's the essence of the loving natural high: when you love something so much it inspires you to work harder to achieve your goals. At the same time, the instructor was engaging in *his* natural high, helping to teach surfing to kids, and it led to inspiring the boy to love surfing. By the way, if you like this anecdote as much as I do, check out the instructor's surf school if you ever get a chance to visit Newport Beach. It's the Endless Sun Surf School (www.endlesssunsurf.com).

When I returned to my hotel room, I quickly posted about the experience on Facebook and got a message from a former fraternity brother of mine, Greg Smith. He was moved by the surfing story because he and his wife have a daughter named Marin who has cerebral palsy. Like the surf instructor, Greg engages in his natural high of running *with* Marin. Greg actually competes in races while pushing her in a modified jogging stroller.

I met Greg for dinner recently and he told me that his training helped him lose 30 pounds and start eating healthier. I can't imagine what it's like to raise a child with a disability, but somehow it seems to have made Greg more resilient. Greg's story inspires me to this day as I follow his activities on social media. In fact, he works with the Kyle Pease Foundation to raise both awareness and funds to help people with disabilities succeed. You can check it out at www.kylepeasefoundation.org.

Pick Your Brain:
The Neurobiology of Helping Others

Human beings have the capacity for being selfish, but they also can show tremendous generosity. The 2006 "Giving USA" survey revealed that, in 2006 alone, over $260 billion was given to U.S. charities, with three-quarters of that money coming from individuals. People give of their time, too. In 2005, over 65 million Americans volunteered to help charities.[1] Almost all volunteers surveyed reported that one of their motivations was "Feeling compassion toward other people." Yet, surprisingly, very little is known about the neurobiology of generosity and helping others.

It may be the case that generosity is part of human behavior because it helps sustain cooperative relationships—which can help ensure survival. In our own lives, perhaps we think that if we give to an organization during their time of need, maybe they'll help us during *our* time of need.

Behavioral scientists have suggested that empathy plays the biggest role in helping behavior. Empathy is the ability to understand someone else's feelings. It's often described as "putting yourself in someone else's shoes." Brain imaging studies in humans have shown that activities involving empathy and charitable giving activate regions in the brain that are known to be active during social and emotional situations, as well as the reward center.[2]

In a recent study, scientists in the Neuroeconomics Studies Department at Claremont Graduate University in California took a unique approach to investigating generosity.[3] They gave study participants a nose spray infused with the neuropeptide oxytocin, which is a neurochemical known to play a role in forming social attachments and feelings of love.

Half of the study participants received oxytocin in the spray and half received a placebo—salt water. Compared to the placebo group, the group that received the oxytocin spray was 80% more generous in a task that involved giving away money to a stranger than those given a placebo. The generous participants left the experiment with less money, but many reported positive feelings associated with their generosity.

These positive feelings are consistent with the effects of oxytocin on the reward center of the brain, which is known to induce dopamine release. If you receive a reward from the brain—in the form of a natural high—by giving, you are more likely to give again.

Similarly, a recent study showed that when people do good things, a part of the brain called the posterior superior temporal cortex (pSTC) is activated.[4] The pSTC governs our altruistic behaviors (i.e., things we do purely for the benefit of others) and perceptions of social relationships. It's believed that some people have a more developed pSTC than others. However, it's not known if those with a highly developed pSTC do selfless things because of how their brain is constructed, or if those doing self-less things develop a more active pSTC. We do know that selfless actions create more of the feel-good chemicals (such as dopamine) in the brain, and the brain is capable of growing and reshaping based on our behaviors.

Try This: Do you want to become a person who helps others or who is simply known as a great listener? You can consciously develop your sense of empathy during conservations by prac-ticing a technique called reflective listening. The idea is to "reflect" back the emotions you sense from the other person as they speak. For example, while listening to a friend rant about something that bothers them, you might say, "That must been really frustrating for you." If you're wrong about the emotion, the person will likely correct you, but will appreciate the concern. If you're right, simply continue to follow their story. Practicing this type of listening shows you're engaged by the story and shows that you care about how they feel.

Learning to Help: Really?

Yes, you can *learn* to be a person who helps others. Even if you weren't raised in a family that valued helping other people, you can overcome that. Neuroscientists believe the brain can be trained to feel empathy for others and to act upon that empathy by helping them. In my opinion, anyone who helps others—particularly helping the less fortunate—needs to receive something from the experience in order to do it again. I'm not talking about money. I'm not even talking about building your resume. If you are truly going to be someone who helps others on a routine basis, feeling something positive from the experience will keep you doing it.

Helping is a natural high. To keep experiencing that high, it's important to engage in helping behaviors on at least a somewhat regular basis. You may not have a flood of feel-good emotions the first or second time you help someone, but making it a routine will increase your chances. Then, maybe when you're least expecting it, you'll receive that natural high that makes it all worthwhile. It may come in the form of an e-mail or a personal "Thank you," but it *will* come back to you. It's nice to know that you're not doing it for that reason, but putting yourself out there will come back in a meaningful way.

Interview: Jamie Sierfeld

Jamie Sierfeld is the director of the Lindsey Meyer Teen Institute, the drug and alcohol prevention and leadership program in New Jersey that I mentioned in the first chapter. Jamie has been with the program since its inception; she started as a student.

In our conversation, she remarked upon on the large numbers of alumni—including myself—who have come through the teen institute program as high school students and continued on to careers in the helping professions (such as teachers, counselors, social workers, and psychologists). The first question I asked was whether she gets a natural high from helping others and if so, what does it feel like?

"I get a natural high from helping people—it feels good," Jamie answered. "For me, the highlight of the year is putting together the week-long leadership conference in August. The natural high comes when I get a chance to stand back and reflect on how we put the entire week together. I know I've had a natural high because I lose track of time and I notice that the little things bother me much less."

I also asked her to talk about how the program can help transform participants into young people who are motivated to help others.

"At the Teen Institute, we see transformations all the time. I'm a good example myself. If I hadn't gotten involved in the Teen Institute of the Garden State—the original name of this prevention and leadership program—there is no way I would have ever chosen this career path. I think the reason so many students go on to work in the helping professions is that the Teen Institute gives concrete examples of what people do in these careers. For example, high school students usually have an abstract idea of what a counselor or social worker does, but when they come to camp and work with these individuals in small groups they see how rewarding it can be."

Helping Is Meaningful Work

"Meaningful work," says bestselling author Malcolm Gladwell, "is one of the most important things we can impart to children. Meaningful work is work that is autonomous. Work that is complex—that occupies your mind. And work where there is a relationship between effort and reward—for everything you put in, you get something out."

I find this quote to be absolutely true and so deeply meaningful in itself. In my opinion, there are few things more meaningful than helping others, especially those less fortunate than you are. For me, helping others means getting in front of groups of students and parents across the country and making them laugh with a message about wellness. For you, perhaps it means checking in on an elderly neighbor, volunteering at an animal shelter, or raising money for medical research. There is inherent meaning in trying to reach out to another human being in need and provide education, assistance, medical service, or just friendship.

Jamie Sierfeld described tremendous meaning behind her work. The Lindsey Meyer Teen Institute is named after a special young woman who participated in the program as a high school student and returned as a youth counselor. That is special enough, but she did all of this while suffering from cystic fibrosis—a rare genetic disease that is life-shortening. Jamie was close friends with Lindsey and knew firsthand what a tremendous impact she had on others.

Lindsey passed away far too young at the age of seventeen. Her wonderful parents took a risk and attempted a double lung transplant, each giving one of their own lungs to her in the hopes it would extend Lindsey's life. She faced the surgery like she faced everything in her life—with a sense of humor and determination.

I remember interviewing Lindsey for the youth counselor position months before the surgery. "There are strict rules for attending the counselor trainings," I told her. "If you miss one, you're out."

She looked at me with these big eyes and said, "I may get a lung transplant soon, which means I may miss some of the trainings. Is that OK?"

Holding back a smile I said, "No, they are very strict. Next question . . ."

"But I need an operation!" she insisted.

"I'm sorry," I said, "it's final." I could only keep a straight face for so long and then we both burst out laughing.

Today, the Lindsey Meyer Teen Institute is part of the Lindsey Meyer Foundation. In Jamie's words: "For me, there is great meaning in working for the Teen Institute. I get to help high school students address problems in their schools and communities, but I also get to give back to Lindsey and her family."

Wrap-Up

Helping others can produce a natural high similar to highs experienced while running, eating, or laughing. Helping behavior can be learned through role models, family, or organizations dedicated to helping others. If you choose a career in the helping professions, you might not be rewarded with a large income, but you will provide yourself with something very special—meaningful work. It has been said that those who love what they do and engage in meaningful work never really work a day in their life.

Chapter 6

Loving, Caring and Other Highs Better Than Hurting Yourself

As an eight-year-old I thought girls were pretty gross and I suspect they didn't think much of me either. It wasn't until the hormones kicked in during the middle school years that I found myself wanting to talk on the phone with girls every night. Up until then the phone was used strictly for ordering pizzas and talking to Nana. Suddenly, in middle school I was compelled to engage in these oddly long conversations with girls about nothing.

When I was in middle school, calling a girl on the phone was an anxiety-filled experience. This may be hard to imagine, but back then there was only one phone in the entire house and it didn't fit in my pocket! To use it, I had to go to the kitchen and if my mother was there, ask to use the phone. Depending on her mood or if she was expecting a call, the entire operation could fail right there. Once I dialed the number, I dashed as far away from the kitchen as the phone cord would allow. I was lucky because we had an oversized cord, which meant I could get three whole feet outside the kitchen before it snapped me back like a rubber band. My mom could still hear me, but for some reason that wasn't nearly as embarrassing as her seeing me talk to girls.

When the phone would ring on the other end, those three to five seconds wondering who was going to answer were the worst seconds of any boy's life. If the girl herself picked up, a feeling of euphoria would wash over me to the point where I wanted to hang up with embarrassment. If it was her mom, I might escape with a short conversation and some sympathy for trying. But if her dad answered the phone, it was always awkward. No father wants to answer that call and no adolescent boy is equipped to deal with that call. It was like watching a deer try to take its first steps and have its legs collapse while a hungry bear looks on.

OK, so here's the point of this little story. As terrible as those early phone experiences were, they forced me to build my social skills. Today, students refer to "talking with someone" when it's usually about "texting someone." Texting, of course, occurs directly with the other person and doesn't involve going through a gatekeeper adult. It's way easier to text, but it's also risky, because you can't hear the *tone* of the person's voice or *see* the expressions on their face. Without getting a clear sense of their reaction, it's hard to really know if they're interested in you or not. As I look back, I wonder why anyone would've gone through the trouble of making those calls, but in those days it was the only option! Besides, the loving natural high can be a big motivator. It was probably more about a crush or infatuation than real love, but it was a powerful natural high nonetheless. The sound of a sweet voice laughing at one of my jokes was a natural high that lasted until my bedtime at 10 PM.

I believe that nature made loving another person one of the most powerful natural highs in existence for one reason—the survival of the species. In my case, I wish someone would have told me in middle school that it would be fifteen years before I had a romantic relationship that would lead to marriage. It would have saved me a lot of phone calls.

The natural high of loving takes three major forms: romantic love, maternal love, and platonic love.

Romantic love encompasses everything from your first crush in school to the 50th wedding anniversary. The natural high of falling in love is so powerful that it can make you do illogical things, like ride your bike twelve miles in the rain just to hang out with a girl named Kristi on a hot summer night. I'm not saying I did that (in August of 1990), but it could happen. The highest highs of romantic love may come during the first few weeks of a new relationship, but the most meaningful highs tend to surface over years of commitment and building a life together. In some cases, romantic love leads to having a baby.

Maternal love—or paternal love for dads—is one of the

strongest motivators of parents to protect their infants. When I wrote the first edition of this book, I couldn't say that I'd experienced paternal love. However, even back then I could appreciate how special it must be because all too often parents will give you 80 reasons why having a child is miserable and then end with "Oh, but I love being a parent so much."

The third loving natural high comes from having an amazing friendship or relationship with a person or pet that is neither romantic nor maternal/paternal. It's one of those relationships that improves the quality of your life and makes you feel great. To me, a great friend is someone you could have fun with while simply waiting in line.

Romantic Love Story

In high school and college, I spent so much time in relationships, trying to get into relationships, or trying to get out of relationships, that you would have thought I was getting credits for it. I'm not sure what the point of all of it was except to prove to myself that I had trouble being alone during those years. It may be the case that I was a little too into the natural high that accompanies new romantic relationships. "Addicted" is too strong a word, because it never interfered with my academics or other activities, but it was certainly a distraction. It's a fact that the novelty of a new relationship is tremendously exciting, but that excitement can work for or against you.

In college, I met another girl named Kristy—with a "y" this time, but not that it matters; I doubt either one will ever read this book. She was a fellow biology student and we met while making photocopies. I guess it was love at first collate. She had big eyes like a Japanese anime cartoon and such a sweet voice that I couldn't resist striking up a conversation. We went out a few times and it was great. We had such a cool chemistry together that each date was more fun than the last. It wasn't long before I found myself having conversations with her about nothing and doing illogical things.

Kristy and I dated for the next year and a half. We had some great times together and even began introducing each other to our families. However, the relationship was complicated by life events—like us attending graduate schools three hours apart and me traveling often. I had a friend who once said, "The right person at the wrong time is still the wrong person." I think Kristy and I met each other at the wrong time, but the illogical romantic love thing still convinced me that she was "the one."

The day Kristy dumped me was like any other. We had been having discussions about transferring graduate schools to live closer to each other, but I could tell that it was not going anywhere. The call came during the afternoon and I was . . . well, I was on the toilet. For some reason, I felt compelled to hobble to the phone, pants around my ankles, and pick up the call. She immediately gave me the "We've got to talk" line.

I was really in no state for a deep conversation, but I was alone so I thought, "Let's do this." She explained that the relationship wasn't working for her and that she needed a break. I don't remember much after that except how short the call was and how quickly it was over forever. I made my way back to the bathroom and with the timing of a comedic actor, I tripped and fell on my sad pathetic face.

It took a few days for the pain to really settle in. When it did I decided to call Kristy for a better explanation (a.k.a., the "try to get back together with her" call). When we dated, we used to call each other every night at 10 PM. It was our time. For the next week, I called at 10 PM and no one answered. I left a message each time and grew increasingly impatient.

Finally, after two weeks, someone picked up the phone. It was a male voice and Kristy lived alone. I asked who it was and he said his name was Matt. The irony of his name was quickly lost on me as I remembered that Kristy had been talking about a Matt who'd started working in her lab. It was him—I was sure of it. I don't know why he was there, but I don't think it was to make coffee.

I left a message and as soon as I hung up completely lost all sense of logic. The natural high of romantic love had become a natural low. I was so crazy that I made plans to blow off the next day and drive three hours that night to see her. Fortunately, a friend talked me down, but the emotional pain of doing nothing was still devastating. Honestly, it felt like someone I loved had died. I felt guilty for feeling that way, but I couldn't control it.

The best advice I was given during that time came from a

movie called *Swingers*. The advice was simple: Do not call, e-mail, or go see this girl ever again—no matter how much it hurts. In time, she will contact you.

I went fourteen months, two weeks, and one day without contacting Kristy—not that I was keeping track. Actually, it was torture. Everything that reminded me of her suddenly became a reason to get depressed. Can you imagine getting bummed out every time you saw a red Ford Focus? I was convinced that I would never be happy again.

One random August day, Kristy contacted me through a mutual friend and asked if we could meet. It almost seemed too similar to the movie. I agreed to get together and I'm glad I did. The meeting was a roller coaster of emotions, but it had a profound effect on my life. When I left I felt as though a weight had been lifted off my chest. I no longer thought Kristy was "the one." I'll always have feelings for her, but on that day it just felt different. She wanted to get back together and I just could not see it. I had been dating someone for a few months and somehow seeing Kristy solidified for me that this new relationship represented the future.

In the weeks following our meeting, I thought about Kristy less and less. It's funny how life works because the girl I was dating at the time eventually became my wife.

Paternal Love Story

My pregnant wife cries a lot, needs to eat every few hours,
and is constantly in the bathroom.
People ask me, "When's the baby due?" and I say, "It's already here."
—Matt Bellace

When I was in college, I gave flowers to a young lady I liked and watched as a look of horror overtook her face. It may have been indigestion, but it was still rejection. I went back to my friends, shared my pain, and they did what good friends do—they made fun of me for three hours. And I actually did feel better. That's love too! You can also love your grandmother, your best friend, and/or your dog. All these forms of love involve a brain chemical called oxytocin. (It's not Oxycontin, by the way. That's a pain pill killing thousands of people.) Oxytocin is an amazing neurotransmitter that gets released when you help someone (the "helper's high") or love someone. Ladies, if and when you give birth, your brain will flood itself with oxytocin. I told that to a group of middle-school girls and they looked at me like, "We're giving birth? I thought that was the guys!" When I saw my wife give birth, my brain flooded itself with fear.

The natural high of childbirth for me happened when we found out we were having a boy. We went to the hospital for an ultrasound and the doctor asked us if we wanted to know if it was a boy or girl right there or later. We opted for later, so the doctor wrote down on piece of paper the gender of our child and we opened it in the lobby of the hospital. We learned that it was a boy and that's when my wife turned to me and said, "I want to name our son after your grandfather who died of cancer." I started crying right there. So we called him "Grandpa." That's unique, right? We have a daughter now. We should have called her "Grandma." Nobody's making out with "Grandma." You'll never hear "Grandma's hot." (Yeah, that's a dad joke.)

My son's real name is Roy. The day I realized just how much I loved him, he was just a little baby and he'd gotten sick for the first time. I raced into his room and everything felt like it was in slow motion. I thought to myself, "This is the first time I've ever run *toward* someone who's vomiting." I picked Roy up and carried him over to the garbage can. Don't judge me! I didn't know where else to go!

When I got to the garbage can, I tried to angle him so that his head was perfectly positioned just above the opening, but his tiny little fingers were tightly gripping the rim and he had the saddest look on his face, like he was afraid I was going to throw him in and kick it down the stairs. I tried to talk logic to a baby: "What are you doing, buddy? I love you!" He just let out a slow-building cry and I felt so helpless. It was at that moment that my brain produced a thought I have never had before. I said to myself, "I would rather be the one throwing up." Now, I *hate* puking. I haven't puked since August 10, 1987. That's one of the benefits of not drinking or doing drugs—you rarely throw up. My love for my son made me put his physical well-being over my vomit-free streak. I found out that paternal love made me want to be a better man.

As I'm writing the new text for this edition, Roy is almost five years old. He constantly tests his limits which, in turn, pushes me to improve myself all the time. The other day, he came up to me holding an action figure made of hard plastic. He looked up and said cheerfully, "Hey Daddy!" Then he threw the action figure as hard as he could, right at my head. I immediately screamed in pain and demanded, "Roy, did you just hit me with that action figure?" Without missing a beat he answered, "No, that was a policeman." Naturally I wanted to strangle him, but instead I turned into Mr. Mackey from *South Park* and said, "That's not what we do, mkay?"

Today, my wife and I have our son Roy and daughter Sidney to love. We are truly blessed with a healthy and (on most days) a happy family. If you can imagine life being incredibly rewarding *and* intermittently aggravating every day, then you can imagine being a parent. I've never loved so deep or yelled so loud. I wouldn't change a thing.

Platonic Love Story

I only knew one of my grandfathers growing up—my mom's father. My dad's father passed away before I was born. So, we affectionately called my mom's father "Pops," and he got all of my attention. Everyone else knew him as Roy Basso—and I do mean everyone. It seemed like everybody who lived within a 20-mile radius of Pops knew him.

The day I learned that my Pops' cancer was terminal I immediately ran into my mother's arms and cried. I was in seventh grade at the time and that was unusual behavior for me. Pops was an iconic figure in my family and he could not be replaced. He had always made me the center of attention when I was around him. In fact, he had put off the CAT scan—which would ultimately diagnose his cancer—by a few days just so we could spend time golfing during my spring break. He was like the glue that held my family together.

Pops had a certain way about him that just seemed to make people want to be near him. I can remember staying with my Nana and Pops on vacation and seeing how much he was in constant social demand. He was the former mayor of Point Pleasant, New Jersey, and owned an Oldsmobile dealership with this brother. As a result, he was able to use his skills to encourage other businessmen to invest in developing the town's boardwalk. Today, that stretch of boardwalk is one of the most popular destinations in the state of New Jersey. I think it's safe to say that his role during that time period helped create what is there today.

I heard so many stories of people helped through hard times by Pops. In some cases, he would loan cars to people in need so they could get a job. People loved my grandfather so much that—unsolicited—they would tell me about it. There would be moments when I would be hanging around the car dealership and some stranger would stop me and say, "Your grandfather Roy is such a special man. I hope you realize." I really did.

One story I always enjoyed was about my grandfather towing cars. Teenagers would drive their cars on the beach and not realize you need to deflate tires to drive over sand, so they would get stuck. Phone calls would come in during the middle of the night begging him for help. I was told that he never accepted money and when asked, "Please don't tell my parents," would always agree. Of course, he knew that it didn't matter if he told or not, because the next time someone went underneath to fix the car, the caked-on sand in the wheel well would give them away every time. I love the story because it demonstrates how much people relied on him for help, but also that he knew to do the right thing.

I can vividly recall sleeping over at my grandparents' house in the final days of Pops' life. I was praying to God and scolding him for allowing this to happen to my grandfather. At one point, I asked that my life be taken so such a great man could be spared. Of course, it was futile. Pops passed away soon after and I was left to make sense of it. Someone I met at the funeral gave me the advice to incorporate my favorite aspects of Pops into my own personality. It was then that I decided that I would do what I could to make a difference in other people's lives, just like Pops did. I have spent the years since pursuing that goal—one that I will never fully complete. As much as I wish I could become Pops, I can only keep him in my memories while I try to be a better version of myself.

While I was in middle school, I decided to wake up each morning and go running to get into better shape. If I didn't feel like doing it one morning, I thought of how courageous Pops was while battling his cancer. In high school, I decided to play three sports—football, wrestling, and baseball. When someone would make fun of me for being too small, too weak, or too white, I would try to emulate Pop's positive attitude. In college, I founded a student prevention group and was told I was committing "social suicide." When the prevention work would get me down, I remembered stories about how courageous Pops was while running for mayor of Point Pleasant. He was the first Italian-American mayor of the town—no small feat in the late 1950s.

Given all of this history, it might not come as a surprise that when my wife and I learned we were going to have a boy, she said to me, "Let's name him after your grandfather because he meant so much to you." It was amazing and wonderful to hear her say those words. The natural high of love for my wife and love for my grandfather came together in that one amazing moment.

Try This: Think about a loved one you've lost. If you are lucky enough not to have lost anyone, then think of someone you admire. Identify one or two positive traits of that individual and ask yourself, "How can I incorporate those traits into my everyday life?" It may surprise you to experience just how great it feels to carry on the memory of a loved one in such a meaningful way.

Pick Your Brain:
Neurobiology of Love

Romantic love, maternal/paternal love, and platonic love are all considered natural highs. They can be highly rewarding experiences that improve mood, energy levels, and feelings of fulfillment. In terms of brain functioning, research suggests that romantic and maternal/paternal love actually activate overlapping regions within the brain's reward system and release feel-good chemicals.

In the case of romantic love, vasopressin, oxytocin, and dopamine have been shown to be released in response to romantic feelings. Maternal love also releases these chemicals, but the brain-activated areas are slightly different (thank goodness). Maternal love produces stronger activation in the part of the brain that's specific for faces. This is consistent with the importance of a mother's ability to read her child's facial expressions and determine how the child is feeling. Interestingly, mothers who give birth without pain medications have been shown to release endorphins, which are morphine-like substances made by the body to relieve pain. Long-distance runners and athletes may also experience this pain but enjoy the runner's high as previously discussed.

Friend and follow psychologist Talia Zaider, Ph.D., gave birth without the use of painkillers and ran a marathon! Thankfully for her child it was not at the same time. I asked her to compare the natural high aspects of the two experiences. "In some ways the high is similar because it's the release you feel from intense and often painful exertion," Talia answered. "Both in completing the New York City Marathon and in giving birth, my body was pushed past any familiar limit and that felt tremendously powerful. The main difference I think is that when I gave birth to Zoe, the high was shared, it enveloped both of us so that we were in total synch. It felt more like the knees-weak feeling of being head over heels in love."

Although it's different than childbirth, you may not be surprised to learn that romantic love can also be an "intense and often painful" experience. For example, you may find yourself obsessed with that person—thinking about them much more than you would normally think about another human being. Well, it turns out that there's a biological basis for that romantic obsession.

An increase in dopamine is often coupled with a decrease in the neurotransmitter serotonin, which is linked to mood. Recent research has shown that serotonin levels in the brains of people who are in love are similar to that of the levels seen in patients with obsessive-compulsive disorder (OCD). The essential features of OCD include recurring obsessions or compulsions that are so severe they take up more than an hour each day and interfere with functioning at work, school, or home.[1] Common compulsions include excessive hand-washing, or elaborate routines performed before leaving the house. For some people, obsessive behavior can make them feel they're reaching their goals, like the student who is hyperfocused on getting into medical school. However, when obsessively thinking about medical school interferes with your performance on a high school exam, then it's becoming a problem.

When it comes to relationships, obsessions can waste time and energy, especially when that love is not returned. Have you ever known someone who has lost a love—whether it's due to breakup or death—and cannot let go of thinking of them? They may talk about the person so much that you ask yourself, "What are they getting from this?"

The grieving process is different for each person. The amount of time needed to heal from this experience may depend on how long you knew the person and the type of relationship. For example, losing a spouse of 50 years will likely entail a much lengthier recovery than grieving after breaking up with a person you dated for six weeks.

The prolonged and enduring pain of losing someone can develop into what is called complicated grief. This used to be referred to as chronic, pathological, or traumatic grief. A recent study found that the brains of individuals who experience complicated trauma show activation in the reward pathways.[2] In fact, some scientists have hypothesized that this type of attachment to the grieving process may have addiction-like properties.[3] While some degree of grieving can be appropriate and healthy, a person must be cautious about falling into a pattern in which they become addicted to the grieving process and the benefits that they may be experiencing from maintaining this process.

One of the ways families and communities respond to death or divorce, for example, is to increase support for those who are hurting. That attention is rewarding, especially for those who've been neglected, abused, or simply have attention-seeking personalities. However, as time passes the attention will inevitably decrease. For some, that will cause them to look for ways to keep the attention coming. One way to do that is to prolong the grieving process longer than expected. It's hard to define that length of time, but again it depends on the nature of the loss. Ultimately, holding on to grief simply to gain attention is not a healthy response.

If you suspect that a friend or loved one fits this description of seeking attention from prolonged grieving, you need to be very careful in approaching the situation. It's difficult to judge another person's pain and you can easily be accused of being insensitive. Encouraging them to join you in an activity that gets them moving, like going for a walk or shopping, can be a great way to start. Another suggestion would be to not respond in conversation to repeated comments. Again, you don't want to be insensitive, but if you've already talked about something, then don't reward the behavior with further attention. Simply change the subject and talk about other topics. The goal is to start showing them other ways to feel good again.

Wrap-Up: Lucky to Love

Compared to other natural highs, the brain has slightly different mechanisms for achieving the high associated with love. That's due to the fact that there are so many different types of loving, including romantic, maternal/paternal, and platonic. The experience of love activates the brain's reward center in all cases, which releases the neurotransmitters vasopressin and oxytocin. The outcome of loving can be intensely positive and rewarding or intensely painful and negative. Obsessing over someone can occur in either case. Yes, the natural high of love is truly unlike any other.

There are so many wonderful books, movies, and songs on the topic of love. My favorite book on platonic love is *Tuesdays with Morrie* by Mitch Albom. I've never been into romantic novels, but some of my favorite romance movies include *Good Will Hunting, Titanic, Slumdog Millionaire,* and *Say Anything* to name a few. My iPod is filled with songs about love. My current favorites include Adele's "Someone Like You," The Fray's "You Found Me," and Kings of Leon's "Use Somebody." There are also tons of nonfiction books and dating websites geared toward seriously helping people find love.

No matter how you find it—or how it finds you—if you are able to experience love in its romantic/platonic/ maternal/paternal forms, now and/or in the future, you should consider yourself quite lucky. In my life, I have known people who have experienced all forms of love and some who seem to have experienced none. I've known miserable people who unfortunately can't appreciate the loved ones in their life, and happy people who seem beloved by all those they meet. I've known parents who seem like they couldn't care less about their children, and married couples who will do anything to have children of their own.

Luck seems to be a big factor in whether or not love finds you, but you are the factor in whether or not you enjoy love. I can tell you that if you are lucky enough to experience the love of a pet, friend, girlfriend, boyfriend, or child, you should not take it for granted. If there are things you've always wanted to do with your loved one, don't put them off. Make plans today to take that trip or have that picnic or just go to a ballgame. Love is to be cherished because time is always a limiting factor in our lives. Loved ones might move away, or grow apart. Loved ones will pass away. What makes love so special is that it is not guaranteed to any of us.

Chapter 7

Unhealthy Natural Highs

A book on natural highs would be incomplete without a chapter about unhealthy natural highs beyond those of alcohol and other drugs. These unhealthy highs are just as likely to be physically and mentally harmful.

It's important to realize that even a natural high activity can be harmful if it's done to excess. For example, running too much can make you dangerously thin and/or excessively preoccupied with exercise. Eating too much can make you obese, and loving someone too much... well, that can make you a stalker.

An unhealthy natural high like gambling or prostitution doesn't have to be illegal to harm you. It doesn't have to involve ingesting a drug. It can make you feel great in the short term, but just like chemical highs, it can cause harm in the long run.

Problem Gambling

Over the years I developed an enormous gambling problem.
I was making 35 grand a week on a sitcom and I was wearing the same
jacket I wore at a Rush concert in 1981.
—Artie Lange

When I was in high school, there were a bunch of guys who started playing a game called "flipping." I don't even remember it well, but I know that it involved throwing pennies against a wall to see who could land the closest to the wall without touching it. It seemed totally random, but a couple of guys I know were completely into it. They would flip every weekend and during lunch if they could find a spot.

I tried it, but never stayed for long because I hated losing money. I guess I'm genetically predisposed to cheapness because the idea of giving away your money and getting nothing for it was painful. However, one of the guys was so into flipping that he began stealing money from his job at 7-Eleven to pay for his gambling.

When he got caught, he was fired from the job, and got into trouble with the police. He was also grounded by his parents, suspended from school, and got kicked off the football team. Other than that he was fine. Looking back at it I'm glad I felt the pain of losing my own money rather than stealing someone else's.

Pathological gambling, or "problem gambling," is considered by psychologists to be what's called an impulse control disorder. One of the main features of impulse control disorders is the failure to resist an impulse or temptation to perform an act that is harmful to the person or others.

Gambling becomes a harmful high once the gambler begins taking greater and greater risks. If someone is willing to lose large sums of money and risk their job and/or relationships just in order to gamble then they have a problem. Gambling is also illegal in most states for people under the age of eighteen. So making it illegal probably intensifies the high of the experience, but doing it instantly makes it a high-risk behavior.

If you suspect that someone may have a problem with gambling, ask yourself the following questions:

Is the person preoccupied with gambling or do they have a need to gamble with increasingly larger amounts of money?

Has the person tried to cut back (unsuccessfully) or do they become restless or irritable when trying to stop?

Is gambling a way for them to escape from their problems?

In addition, does the person lie, commit illegal acts, and/or risk significant relationships, all to keep their gambling habit going?

Finally, does the person rely on others to provide them with money to relieve desperate financial situations caused by gambling?

If you're answering "yes" to several of these questions, it's time to encourage the person to seek professional help.

In recent years there's been a dramatic increase in the availability of gambling options in the United States. Internet gambling has basically turned the home computer into a slot machine. For a problem gambler, the internet is available around the clock and can be like a loaded gun.

Problem gambling is believed to affect 1–2% of the U.S. population. A random telephone survey that was recently conducted with over 2,000 U.S. residents 14–21 years old revealed that 68% of respondents had gambled in the past year and 11% gambled at a frequency of twice per week.[1] These young people could be in training to become the problem gamblers of tomorrow.

The good news is that if you need to seek help for yourself, a friend, or loved one, there is hope. There are two common forms of treatment for problem gamblers: Gamblers Anonymous (GA) and cognitive behavioral therapy (CBT).

GA (www.gamblersanonymous.org) provides support groups for those with gambling addictions. There's not a lot of research about how effective the GA programs are. Nonetheless, GA is a kind of self-help treatment that's free of charge, and is often the only treatment option available in many communities. GA meetings can be found in most residential treatment programs and local community centers.

In contrast, CBT is a professional form of treatment conducted by a clinical psychologist in both individual and group settings. CBT focuses on the thoughts, behaviors, and feelings that trigger and maintain the behaviors associated with gambling. To find a CBT-trained psychologist, you can visit www.aabt.org.

One recent study found that there were no significant differences in treatment success when comparing CBT and GA.[2] Overall, participants who attended more sessions—regardless of whether it was part of a GA or CBT program—tended to achieve better outcomes than those who didn't undergo any intervention for their problematic behaviors.

In light of the increasing prevalence of problem gambling, more research is clearly needed in order to determine the most effective treatment for those struggling with this often debilitating disorder.

Pick Your Brain:
Problem Gambling and Dopamine

The brain chemical dopamine plays a major role in the reward system of both humans and animals. Any behavior that makes you feel good and makes you want to engage in the behavior again likely involves dopamine. When someone goes to a casino and wins, they'll experience positive feelings. The next time that person thinks about gambling, they're more likely to do it since the behavior has been reinforced by the positive feelings of winning money.

In neuroscience, we often learn about the way healthy brains work by looking at brains that are diseased. For example, recent studies have shown that patients with Parkinson's disease—a degenerative disease of the brain that reduces dopamine levels and impairs muscle functioning—are also more likely to develop gambling problems.[3]

The superficial conclusion might be that these patients are "giving up on life" and "going for broke" at the casinos. However, it turns out that there is actually a connection between Parkinson's, gambling, and a drug used to treat the disease.

One type of drug used to treat Parkinson's is called a dopamine agonist. This is basically a class of drugs that mimics the effect of dopamine in the brain and helps alleviate some of the symptoms of the disease. However, the administration of a dopamine agonist has been shown in recent studies to cause patients in their 50s and 60s with no prior history of gambling problems to start gambling.

These patients report that they engage in high-risk gambling—sometimes losing thousands of dollars—and have no real explanation for why they started. Interestingly, when the dopamine agonist is reduced, the gambling problem subsides. Researchers studying this issue don't know exactly why the medication is influencing a gambling behavior, but let's hope the casinos don't found out!

Overeating

I was just in Las Vegas and I lost a lot of money. But I get 'em back at the buffet— $9.95 all you can eat. We'll see who wins at this hand.
I got to the prime rib table and said, "Hit me."
—John Pinette

The natural high of eating has an ugly cousin called overeating. It's also known as binge eating or simply eating too much in any one sitting. Binge eating is defined as eating within two hours or less (for some it takes only ten minutes) what most people would consider to be a large amount of food, while experiencing a sense of loss of control. This loss of control is typically described as feeling as though it's difficult to stop eating, and/or to control what or how much you're eating.

Those who have engaged in overeating and/or binge eating for many years are often seriously overweight and referred to as obese, morbidly obese, or even "super obese." The latter term makes it sound like the person is some sort of eating superhero.

The problem is that overeating has become an epidemic in our country as many individuals have difficulty maintaining reasonable portion control. Overeating costs people money, quality of life, and health. Scientists believe that there are similarities between overeating and drug addiction. In fact, the neurochemical dopamine has been suggested to have a common role in drug abuse and obesity.[4]

According to the Centers for Disease Control and Prevention, 16% of U.S. children (that's over 9 million) from the ages of six to nineteen years old are overweight or obese—a number that has tripled since 1980. Overweight adolescents have a 70% chance of becoming overweight or obese adults. This risk increases to 80% if one or more parents of an individual is overweight or obese.[5]

This alarming rate of obesity is a major problem because of its implications for the health of Americans. Obesity increases the risk of many diseases and health conditions, including:
- Coronary heart disease
- Type 2 diabetes
- Cancers (endometrial, breast, and colon)
- Hypertension (high blood pressure)

- Dyslipidemia (high total cholesterol or high levels of triglycerides)
- Stroke
- Liver and gallbladder disease
- Sleep apnea and other respiratory problems
- Osteoarthritis (degeneration of cartilage and its underlying bone)
- Gynecological problems (for example, abnormal periods, infertility)

In a study that looked at the economic impact of childhood obesity from 2002–2005, obese children required $194 more in annual outpatient doctor visit expenditures, $114 more in annual prescription drug expenditures, and $12 more in annual emergency room expenditures compared to children of average weight.[6] When these data are applied to the entire child population in the country, children with an elevated body mass index (a calculation using height and weight to determine body fat) would be associated with $14.1 billion in additional prescription drug, emergency room, and outpatient visit costs annually. I never realized obesity was such a big profit maker for hospitals. I'm thinking if these children suddenly lost weight the government would have to bail out more than just McDonald's.

Unfortunately, too many people choose to treat their problem of overeating with another extreme measure—fad dieting. A diet is flawed from the start because it typically involves making changes to one's eating habits that aren't sustainable over the long term.

A recent study published in the *New England Journal of Medicine* looked at the outcomes of dieters using various different fad diets, such as Atkins or the Zone diet.[7] Each diet touts its own combination of fat-to-carbohydrate intake ratios. The results suggested that reduced calorie diets, regardless of what types of nutrients they emphasize, showed consistent weight loss.

Ultimately, the ratio of calories you take in to calories you burn in a given day is the most important factor that determines whether an individual will lose weight over time. Of course, you should always speak to your doctor before beginning any weight-loss program.

The most tragic aspect of obesity is the loss of quality of life.

A friend of mine was morbidly obese for most of his life. From a natural highs perspective, it was hard—even impossible—for him to enjoy active natural highs like running, biking, or surfing. In fact, even walking—especially in warm weather—was such a nuisance for him because he would sweat so much. Eventually he needed gastric bypass surgery to save his life because for him, diet and exercise were not enough.

Since the surgery, he has lost a considerable amount of weight and increased his activity level, which is quite admirable. However, his successful surgery also resulted in some difficult aftereffects. He is now faced with a skin reduction surgery to tighten all the loose skin. He also experiences a constant struggle not to overeat—and it's easy to overeat when your stomach is a quarter of its original size! In addition, the surgery itself unfortunately did not teach my friend what it means to consume moderate portions of appropriate foods.

He and I had dinner a while back at a great pizza place near his home. He was over two years post-surgery and overall doing well. At the meal, though, he ate what was a normal amount for me, but it was a little too much for him, and on the way he home had some gastrointestinal distress. I normally would not kid about someone's medical condition, but he has such a great sense of humor about his diarrhea that I had to share.

We were driving through the city streets at the time when he alerted me to his situation. I tried to lighten the mood and asked him, "How far along are you?" As someone with irritable bowel syndrome, I tend to classify my own situations based on the Defcon System.

Defcon 5 would indicate a normal, peaceful bowel situation. Defcon 4 would indicate a normal, but heightened bowel alert— the typical post-meal grumbling. Defcon 3 is a state of increased readiness to evacuate. In my mind you've got fifteen to twenty minutes tops until detonation. Defcon 2 requires immediate action toward the proper facilities. Time is of the essence and there is little room for error. When Defcon 1 is reached, you'd better be in on the throne or near a pizza box. It is beyond the point of no return.

Well, he was at Defcon 3 and we were about 30 minutes from home. I pleaded with him, "Stop off at a Starbucks or Dunkin' Donuts. Why stress?"

He looked at me and said, "No, I have a thing about public bathrooms."

As he slipped closer to Defcon 2, I could see the sweat beading on his forehead. We passed a California Pizza Kitchen and I screamed, "Just go in. Don't be a hero!" We both burst out laughing, which was not helpful. He was able to make it home in time, but it must be tough to live a life in fear of being too far from a decent bathroom.

Everyone's relationship with food is complicated. We all need to eat to survive, but we need to be aware that food can also make us sick. A hundred years ago, healthy eating used to mean just having lots of food to eat. Today, we understand so much more about the difference between high-nutrient foods and low-nutrient foods. However, now more than ever, we need to understand the difference because there are so many sources of unhealthy foods that are cheap and readily available.

Keep in mind that simple boundaries can be a great way to prevent overeating. If you consume two or three sodas a day, try drinking only one. You'll probably enjoy it more and you'll eliminate a ton of sugar from your diet. Eating food with the least amount of processing will make a big difference. Processed foods often contain lots of salt and other preservatives that natural foods do not. Those additives are just that—they add weight and don't give you much nutritional value. Plus, you'll feel better about the food knowing it's high in nutrients. Finally, be mindful of the amount of food you eat and how it makes you feel. You may find that a portion of your intake comes *after* you're aware of feeling full.

Excessive Exercising

My first time working out I had no idea what I was doing.
This guy at the gym asked, "So, what are you working out?"
I said, "Childhood issues. Is there a machine for that?"
—Ted Alexandro

Exercise—like most natural highs—can be abused when it is done to excess. How is "excessive" defined? Well, research psychologists use four criteria:

1) Exercising more than two hours per day and having distress if unable to exercise
2) Exercise causes significant interference with important activities
3) Frequent exercise at inappropriate times and places and little or no attempt to suppress the behavior, and/or
4) Exercising despite more serious injury, illness or medical complications.

Excessive exercise tends to be associated with eating disorders—like anorexia nervosa or bulimia nervosa—which are among the deadliest of the psychiatric conditions.[8]

Physical activity brings about so many positive changes for the brain, including growth of neurons in the hippocampus (the brain structure needed for memory), improved cognitive functions, and increased circulation. However, excessive exercise was recently shown to increase anxiety-like behaviors in mice.[9] I'll admit the concept of studying anxiety in mice sounds like a joke. How can you be sure a mouse is anxious? Is he talking nonstop about traps or refusing to leave his hole in the wall?

It turns out that scientists have a couple of objective measures for studying anxiety in a mouse, including measuring their willingness to walk in an open, well-lit area and/or explore a maze. When allowed to run on a wheel for many hours (mice love running wheels), the mice showed less interest in exploring the open field or the maze compared to the mice who were not allowed to run as much.

The scientists interpreted the lack of interest (such as standing still next to a wall) as anxiety-related behavior. If you're curious, they did make sure to control for fatigue so that the mice weren't just worn out and not walking! It's difficult to generalize the results of a study on mice to human behavior, but these findings suggest that more research is warranted to examine the connection between excessive exercise and anxiety.

As I mentioned earlier, my wife is a clinical psychologist who specializes in the treatment of eating disorders. Based on what I've learned from her, I'm aware that a comprehensive discussion of eating disorders could fill this entire book and then some. For the purposes of our discussion, it is important to realize the difference between normal exercise and over-exercise.

Exercise can be a terrific way to strengthen muscles, improve circulation, and elevate mood, but when it's used solely to purge the body of excess calories or to compensate for eating certain foods it is a problem. Excessive exercise is most common among the purging subtype of anorexia nervosa.[9] However, individuals who are of a normal weight or even somewhat overweight can also engage in this problematic behavior.

Over-exercising may go unnoticed at first, but after a few months—as the person loses more and more weight—they begin to look unhealthy. A malnourished person can have pale skin, thin and brittle hair, and a sunken look to their face. They may try to hide their thinness with oversized shirts or big glasses. You may notice unusual things like they always seem to be at the gym and their workouts may consist of significant amounts of time spent on cardio equipment (for example, the treadmill or elliptical machine). They may also go through an amazing quantity of sneakers.

A 1999 study reported that more than half of 5th through 12th grade girls were unhappy with their body weight and shape, and that the unhappiness often resulted in dieting to lose weight and exercising to lose weight.[10] Glamour magazines, television, and the internet often portray images of young women who look perfect and almost impossibly thin. These images are often altered and airbrushed to remove blemishes and body fat, but the viewer is not aware of this. The implicit message to young women is this: if you don't look like these images then you are not attractive.

This is incredibly unfortunate because many of these young women and some young men will begin dieting and exercising to extremes in an effort to achieve a look that is not even possible in real life.

If you know someone who has a problem with over-exercising or who you think may have an eating disorder, there is help available. There are treatment centers that specialize in diagnosing and treating individuals with eating disorders. A good treatment center for eating disorders tends to take a multidisciplinary approach, with psychiatrists, psychologists, nutritionists, and other medical professionals on staff.

Ideally, the treatment facility should consist of specialized inpatient and outpatient services so that each phase of an individual's treatment can be provided in a comprehensive manner.

Many academic medical centers tend to provide this level of specialized, responsible care for individuals struggling with eating disorders. In addition to providing state-of-the-art care, they are often conducting treatment studies which provide treatment free of charge if you qualify. For more information, please visit www.edreferral.com.

High-Risk Sexual Behavior

Tiger Woods always gives 110%. That's why he gave 100% to his wife, but still had 10% left over for his mistresses.
—Steven Colbert

Sex is a natural high and the brain rewards itself for having sex by releasing feel-good neurotransmitters. Scientists believe that the evolutionary reason sex feels good is to increase the chances that humans will continue to seek it out to reproduce and keep the species going.

The chapter on "Loving" focuses on the natural high of not just sex, but love. As simple as the natural high of sex may be, the act of really loving someone and maintaining a relationship is anything but simple. One obvious example of this is the number of stories on the news about young people who thought they were being flirtatious by sexting (i.e., sending nude pictures of themselves to someone) and ended up completely embarrassed or, worse, in trouble.

It's not any easier for older people either. It seems like every week we see a new celebrity or politician get busted for an extramarital affair, putting the natural high of sex over the natural high of loving their long-term partner. Of course, the frequency of commercials for male erectile dysfunction or articles about low female sexual desire make you wonder how older people even have the desire for one relationship, let alone more. But when it comes to high-risk sexual behavior, the threat is more than just your reputation or relationships; it can be physically and mentally harmful.

Nationwide, 16.2%, or about one out of six people 14 to 49 years of age, are infected with the sexually transmitted disease herpes simplex virus-2, which causes genital herpes. In New York

City, more than one-fourth of adults are infected with genital herpes. This is concerning—not just because it's nasty, but because it facilitates the spread of the HIV virus. Genital herpes is sexually transmitted and its symptoms include genital ulcers or sores and even infections of the brain.

The individuals in the survey who contracted sexually transmitted diseases may not have been aware that they were participating in high-risk sexual behavior when they contracted their disease. You don't have to be paying a prostitute for sex or have unprotected sex with a stranger to be engaging in high-risk sexual activity. There are many forms of high-risk sexual activity that involve things you may not have previously considered.

For example, having sex with someone who is emotionally abusive to you is a high-risk sexual behavior because it may cause psychological pain. The pain may not even come during the act, but rather later when you learn they were cheating on you or spreading rumors about you. Having sex while under the influence of alcohol and other drugs can increase a person's risk-taking behavior.

As a student at Bucknell University, I was a member of a fraternity. I was only a member for two years, but it was an eventful time in my development. One night, our fraternity had a mixer with their favorite sorority. One of our pledges proceeded to get drunk and "hook up" with one of the similarly drunk sorority sisters. This was so commonplace at the time that very few people even noticed that night. Apparently, the two ended up back in the dorm in either his or her room and they had sex.

The next morning, the young woman pressed charges, claiming that she'd been passed out and didn't consent to having sex. The young man denied this and claimed that the sex was consensual. The case was brought up in both the local court and within the campus judicial system. The local court threw out the case because both parties admitted to being so drunk they couldn't remember many details of the evening. The Bucknell campus judicial system, however, ruled in favor of the young lady and expelled our pledge. The young woman later found out that she was pregnant, continued on at school, had the baby, and put it up for adoption. I don't know what happened to our pledge. He left school and I have never heard from him again.

The Choking Game

It's known by many other names: the "pass-out game," "blackout," "flatliner," or "suffocation roulette." The object is the same: choking yourself or having a friend do it for you, passing out, and reviving—waiting for that ten-second high as oxygen rushes back into the brain. The most common age range for kids playing this game is between nine and fourteen years old.

During my clinical psychology internship I treated a 60-year-old gentleman for memory loss. He was otherwise in good health, but he was complaining of increased problems with organization, short-term memory loss, and irritability. He reported that his memory was "never good," but had worsened over the past year and it was frustrating for him.

There was no history of Alzheimer's disease in his family and no risk factors for vascular dementia. (Vascular dementia is the second most common form of dementia, caused by chronic reduction in blood flow to the brain as the result of a stroke or series of strokes.) The results of his cognitive testing revealed a profile more similar to someone with a head injury. I had already asked him about a history of concussions, car accidents, or falls and he reported nothing. My supervisor encouraged me to go back and ask more questions about his childhood.

As soon as I did, this patient informed me that during middle school he played the choking game more times than he could remember. It would occur during recess or after school when no adult supervision was present. A friend would press him against a wall until he would pass out, and then he would usually wake up within a few seconds. He had never thought that the game could cause brain damage that could impact his memory 50 years later.

In December 2008, an article about my presentations on natural highs appeared in a number of newspapers across the country. As a result, I was contacted by Lyndi Trost, a grandmother who lost her thirteen-year-old grandson Braden in 2005. Braden and his friends had been playing the choking game, when it turned deadly. Lyndi noted that there are hundreds of other young victims like her grandson, especially when we consider the number of young people who could sustain brain damage from the activity without even knowing it at the time.

It's her personal mission, Lyndi told me, to "make sure that every child, beginning in elementary school, is educated about the dangers of the choking game." She contacted me in the hopes that I would help spread the word. Here in this book, I've kept my promise to Lyndi. I feel terrible for her loss.

Pick Your Brain:
Anoxia

It's impossible to predict the amount of brain damage that can result from playing the choking game. Brain scanners tend to be better at locating specific areas of brain damage rather than generalized cell death across the brain. In addition, it's hard to know exactly how the brain's health may be compromised over the course of a person's life, such as those caused by breathing in environmental toxins or a chronic lack of sleep.

However, it's a fact that we only get one brain in our lifetime and injuries to it are cumulative. Each time a person passes out, brain cells die off. The process is called "anoxia," which literally means "without oxygen." The area of the brain most affected by anoxia is the memory center of the temporal lobe.[11,12] The memory center is a collection of brain structures that happens to be adjacent to the largest supply of blood entering the brain—the middle cerebral artery. When a person passes out, there's a disruption of blood flow through the middle cerebral artery and cells are immediately impacted. If anoxia lasts longer than a few seconds, that person can die.

If you're concerned that someone you know might be involved in the pass-out game, here are some warning signs: bloodshot eyes, unusual marks on the neck, belts and ropes found with unusual knots found tied to furniture. For more information about the choking game go to: www.gaspinfo.com.

Cutting

Highs come in many forms. Some create a sense of happiness and euphoria, while others reduce tension and produce a sense of calm. Chemical highs, like those resulting from the use of

Valium or marijuana, have been reported to reduce anxiety and produce a sense of well-being. Natural highs, like a vacation at the ocean or the mountains, can also produce the same sense of well-being.

However, there is also an unhealthy natural high known as cutting that can create a feeling of reduced tension and calm. On May 6, 2008, the *New York Times* published these descriptions of cutting in an article by Jane E. Brody:

"I feel relieved and less anxious after I cut. The emotional pain slips away into the physical pain. It [cutting] expresses emotional pain or feelings that I'm unable to put into words."

Cutting is not well understood, partly because it is such a secretive activity. Cutting typically occurs in adolescents or young adults, and it tends to be a response to feelings of anger, abuse, or neglect.[13] Experts estimate that this type of self-injury is practiced by 15% of the general adolescent population. The individual generally reports feeling extremely tense, anxious, or angry prior to self-mutilation, while a sense of relief, calm, or satisfaction follows. Occasionally these individuals also report feeling guilty or disgusted after cutting themselves.[14]

It is important to note that cutting is not a form of attempted suicide. Instead, cutting appears to be a dysfunctional attempt to manage emotions by seeking a sensation that will distract the individual from intense emotions. Unfortunately, these people have difficulty coping appropriately with their emotions, thereby resorting to extremely unhealthy and risky behaviors as a maladaptive way to cope (or, really, not cope) with such feelings.

I was reading somewhere that cutting is a socially unacceptable form of self-injury. Then the non-psychologist part of my brain thought, "Are there socially acceptable forms of self-injury?" Of course, how could I forget tattoos, tongue rings, and various other ways to get back at your parents. However, sometimes those little rebellions come back to haunt you. That Tom Cruise tattoo seemed like a great idea after *Top Gun*, but then came *Eyes Wide Shut* and Oprah's couch and now all you've got is a scar of Tom's head and hepatitis C.

Cutting is different than getting a tattoo or piercing you might regret later. Cutting tends to be a repetitive self-mutilation of the body—typically on the wrists and arms—and is often done with a razor blade. It's harmful on many levels, but the most damaging is that it prevents an individual from developing healthy coping mechanisms to deal with life's stresses. It is theorized that cutting releases opiate-like endorphins in the brain that result in a high state and subsequent emotional relief.

The treatment for cutting involves a relatively new psychological intervention called dialectical behavior therapy (DBT). DBT is a treatment designed specifically for individuals who engage in self-harming behaviors, as well as those who experience suicidal thoughts and attempts. DBT is a modified form of CBT discussed earlier (see "Problem Gambling" section on page 150). Medication for stabilizing mood can also be a part of some treatment plans, as many people experience underlying depression or anxiety that may contribute to their behaviors.

Excessive Video Game / Internet Use

For Christmas, all I wanted was this video game called Atari.
I never got it. Instead, I got Adari.
He was an exchange student. Nice guy, but not as good as the game.
—Matt Bellace

In college, there were these computer labs that were open 24 hours a day. I always knew that at some point during the semester, I was going to end up there writing a paper at two o'clock in the morning. Almost every time I went to this one lab, the same two guys were sitting there. It could be midnight or three in the morning, but there they were. They had that "we've never found a soap we've liked" look about them. By the fourth time I saw them there, I realized that they were not working in the traditional sense. They were doing what my friends called "electronic crack"—playing video games.

Their game of choice involved something known as MUD or MUDing. "MUD" stands for Multi-Loser—I'm sorry... Multi-*User* Domain. Here I am making fun of them. These guys could be running a division of Microsoft right now on their own island in the Pacific. The truth is the concept was actually pretty revolutionary at the time because many players could simultaneously compete without having to sit in the same room. The games were text-based and helped spawn some of the wildly popular games of today like World of Warcraft and Second Life.

I love video games. I forged many friendships in middle school, high school, and college around joysticks. All right, that was a bad choice of words. Let me start over. Video games are the only thing that can make you angry at a sunny day because you can't see the screen. The moment I beat Mike Tyson in Mike Tyson's Punch-Out, I was grinning like I was about to get paid for it.

Unfortunately, any activity that you do so much it interferes with your relationships, schoolwork, or job can be bad for you. I didn't get to know those two guys in the college computer lab. Yet I suspect they couldn't help but play games all night and probably neglected their schoolwork. At the very least they neglected their shampoo.

Video games interfered with my own grades at one point during college. I was a sophomore at Bucknell and found myself in a depressing situation. I had gone away to school thinking baseball would be my first priority. I thought that college would be the best four years of my life socially. But two years in, I was seeing no playing time on varsity and my social life was like the movie *Groundhog Day*: every party was the same. Drunk people, sticky floors, an aroma of puke and beer, and lots of loud people more interested in drinking than talking.

Video games eventually became a great outlet for me and seemed like a very social experience. There were always guys hanging out willing to play and no parents to tell you to stop. In a way, video games became my coping mechanism when I didn't know how to handle a reality that didn't measure up to my expectations.

Yet video games are really an altered reality. They exist as an alternative to the real world. The simple act of playing a video game is not unhealthy. It's the repetitive use of the games that can interfere with one's life. If the video games are serving as the main coping mechanism in a person's life, then the video game use only increases if life becomes more stressful.

This type of video game use can also become socially isolating, which can often keep someone from seeking the kind of social support that they may really need during difficult times.

In 2007, the American Medical Association decided not to recommend to the American Psychiatric Association that they include internet addiction as a formal diagnosis in the 2012 edition of the *Diagnostic and Statistical Manual of Mental Disorders.* Instead, they recommended further research on "video game overuse." I suspect it will become a formal diagnosis at some point. As soon as doctors who grew up in the video game and internet era start to run the American Psychiatric Association, the thinking will likely become more progressive.

In my opinion, there is no question that using video games and the internet can be a lot of fun. Like many other behaviors, when done in moderation, it's a form of a natural high. Yet when it becomes a compulsion that interferes with normal functioning in school or at work, it becomes psychologically unhealthy.

Dangerous Risk Taking

If you are attacked by a grizzly bear and you're not the Man vs. Wild guy, you'll probably have a tremendous surge of the neurotransmitter called epinephrine. It's also known as adrenaline and it's involved in the "fight or flight" response. Of course, the Man vs. Wild guy probably stays calm, drinks his own urine, and talks the bear down.

Yet when most average human beings are confronted with a grizzly, they want to jump out of their shoes and run away as fast as they can. Epinephrine intensifies your ability to concentrate and can even cause you to perform acts of strength that amaze you. (Oh, and by the way, playing dead is supposed to be better at fending off a bear attack because bears are used to chasing their food.)

The term "adrenaline junkie" was used in the 1991 movie *Point Break* and refers to people who engage in dangerous activities just for the adrenaline rush. We tend to think of extreme sports when the term "adrenaline rush" comes to mind. We can picture some guy getting dropped onto the top of a mountain by a helicopter and skiing down, or even better—surfing a monster wave.

These are extreme examples of people who put themselves into harm's way and have the training to do so, and/or just have a daredevil inside of them that believes they can survive the risk and get out alive. For example, there was a *60 Minutes* story about young men who free-fall off of fjords in Norway using nothing but suits designed to catch wind and a small parachute. It was an awe-inspiring video, seeing these birdmen base-jumping. On the one hand, it's an example of uplifting the human spirit by pushing the limits of what we think is possible. On the other, it's about people with a compulsion to risk everything for the ultimate natural high. In fact, the story reported that a man had died during one of their previous jumps.

As an adventure-loving guy, I understand there is risk in every activity. However, the concept that even the slightest mistake will cost a life seems extremely rigid for a recreational activity. These are not Navy Seals dropping into enemy territory to save hundreds of lives. I think this is where the "junkie" part of the phrase "adrenaline junkie" comes into play. When someone is willing to lose their job, money, family, or even their life for their sports, that is out of balance.

The National Football League—and every football league, for that matter—is trying to respond to research that links concussions with dementia later on in life. Within the past few years, high school, college, and pro teams have all instituted pre- and post-concussion testing with strict guidelines for return to play. However, head injuries and deaths continue to be a risk of playing football—and other contact sports.

Some argue that the improvement in helmet safety has actually made players more reckless hitters. However, a big part of the problem is that many players who sustain concussions don't want to come out of games. In graduate school, I tested a high school football player who had sustained multiple concussions. The testing revealed that he was having memory and other cognitive problems, so we recommended that he sit out the rest of the season. I will never forget the resistance from the father and son when we made our recommendation. It was like we were suddenly the enemy instead of experts trying to help.

The salary and attention given to professional athletes has become so out of balance compared to the average person that it provides huge incentives for young players to risk it all. Sports can be a natural high, but like anything else there is a fine line between the healthy and the unhealthy. Lying to continue playing with a head injury is an indication that the compulsion to keep playing is more important than healthy safety.

A far more common—and far less interesting—form of an adrenaline junkie is people addicted to drama. These people tend to love arguments, fights, and crises, and are generally always living under some sort of pressure. This type of activity produces the stress response. Epinephrine is released as a short-term response to stress, along with a chemical called cortisol. Cortisol increases your blood pressure and suppresses your immune system to allow you to focus all of your energy on the problem at hand. That may explain why so many students living under pressure during final exams end up getting sick.

Johnny Drama is one of the main characters in the HBO series *Entourage*. Even in the best of circumstances, Drama finds a reason to be anxious, angry, or just unhappy. We've probably all known a Johnny Drama, but we may not have realized that they were getting a natural high from the conflict. But it's an unhealthy natural high, since long-term exposure to this type of stress can cause a host of physical and psychological problems, like cancer, heart disease, and depression.

Try This: The Johnny Drama personality may be fun to watch, but it can be a harmful way of life. Practicing relaxation techniques is a great way to reverse the body's stress response. These techniques can be as simple as breathing slowly and deeply when you're feeling overwhelmed, leaving the room when you're feeling angry, or removing yourself from a chronically stressful situation.

The technique that works best for me is reframing a situation. The idea is not to compound your external stress (for example, a car accident) with internal stress ("My car insurance will now be so expensive I won't be able to afford it!"). Once I've come up with one or two alternative perspectives that are more objective or even positive, I tend to refocus and can calm down.

When you're stressed, it can be difficult to come up with alternate ways to look at a situation. This is when your support network of friends and family can really help out. I'm fortunate to have a wife who is a highly skilled at reframing things. One night at dinner, I was feeling down about not performing as much stand-up comedy in clubs as I used to. My brain was producing negative thoughts like "I'm not working hard enough. I'll never get better," but Dara simply said, "Maybe you're doing fewer comedy clubs because you're so busy speaking at schools?" She also reminded me that I once told her how speaking to students was far more fulfilling than any comedy show at a club. I found the conversation to be helpful because it reminded me to appreciate the great things that I have rather than the things I don't have. I still think about some of her comments whenever my brain wanders into that negative territory.

The next time you're faced with a situation that causes negative thoughts and internal stress, try writing out a few reframed thoughts. If you find it difficult, then ask a friend or loved one to help you brainstorm alternative thoughts. It costs nothing—and just might help you feel better.

Wrap-Up

Unhealthy natural highs can be as destructive as any chemical high. A problem gambler, chronic cutter, or person suffering from an eating disorder experiences stress on their health and their relationships. The fact that a drug is not being taken can obscure the reality that the brain can react *as if* a drug has been taken. This is a fairly new idea, even for neuroscientists. Fortunately, there are effective treatments for behavioral addictions, such as DBT for cutting or Gamblers Anonymous for gambling problems.

When thinking about the healthy version of natural highs, remember that a key element is balance. When an activity becomes more important than health, safety, or anything else, a sense of life balance has been compromised. Healthy natural highs should be the antidote to stress, not the cause of it. They should fit into your life in a way that seems to enhance how you feel about everything else.

Chapter 8

Creating Your Own Natural High

I decided in fourth grade that I wanted to be a doctor, but I had no idea what type. My only problem was figuring out how I'd fit in all the schoolwork while also playing shortstop for the New York Yankees. Fortunately, Derek Jeter came along and made it easier for me to focus on the doctor thing. I received a Ph.D. in clinical psychology from Drexel University in June 2005, 21 years after the fourth-grade daydream. Receiving a doctoral degree after so many years was one of the most intense natural highs I've ever experienced. I was giddy to the point of being annoying to others around me. And one key reason it was so intense was because of all the obstacles that seemed to stand in the way during my journey.

As a freshman at Bucknell University, I failed my first biology test. I got a 38 out of 100. To make matters worse, I had a friend who dropped out of the class because he got a 68 and didn't think he could pick his grade up enough to do well. If you're thinking it sounds like a hard class, it really wasn't. It was considered "baby bio," which meant that it was a class for non-biology majors. Real biology majors thought it was a joke, which was unfortunate because at the time I failed the test I was thinking of majoring in biology. I guess when it rains, it pours.

There were two roads I could have taken after getting the 38. I could've dropped the class and given up any dreams of majoring in biology. The other move was to study constantly and just try to really learn the subject. I chose to stick it out and spent countless hours in the library. I studied harder than I ever had before and I ended up getting a C+ for the semester—not bad, considering. I was no Rhodes Scholar and my GPA would never impress anyone, but those days taught me that no matter how down I was, hard work made a difference. Biology had been something I loved learning about since the whole spider plant project in third grade. So why should I give it up just because I wasn't perfect?

Eventually I took enough biology classes to qualify for the major. During those classes, I watched the cutthroat premed students fight to get their A minuses bumped up. One student was so excited he actually yelled out loud, "I got it up to a 97!" Meanwhile, his entire face would twitch because of nervous tics. I wanted to tell him, "Dude, getting an A is not worth making my face look like that."

The truth is I had some real anxiety of my own. Each exam in the higher levels of biology revealed my psychological weaknesses. I worked harder and harder, but when it came time for the tests I kept blowing questions on material that I had in fact studied. I think it was because I was completely distracted by everything in the room. This one guy was so nervous he used to chew his nails like a dog chewing a bone. It would make this disgusting, wet, popping sound. I would've said something, but he was such a nice guy I felt bad. This other girl used to finish the tests in half the time it took everyone else to finish, and then she would make a lot of noise while leaving the room. What an attention-seeking pain-in-my-butt move! There is nothing more demoralizing than struggling on question number two while Usain Bolt over there is zipping up her bag.

Things got so bad that I eventually went to a psychologist on campus to talk about my struggles. His name was Dr. Eric Afsprung and he had the quietest office I'd ever been in. He was such a calming person that I couldn't think of a better psychologist to soothe my weary nerves.

At first, we discussed whether or not it could be a learning disability. Of course, my mind went right for the self-defeating "I'm just not smart enough to be here" angle. What a waste of mental energy. It turns out neither one was likely. As we explored things further, it seemed clear that it was my test-taking anxiety that was affecting my scores.

Dr. Afsprung wrote a letter to my professors asking them if I could take my exams in a quiet room. As soon as I did, my grades went up and suddenly I felt better about my academic performance. It's amazing that a simple change of room could change my grades.

The semester that I saw Dr. Afsprung was also the semester I took a class that would change my career. It was called Physiological Psychology and it focused on how the nervous system functions from the cellular level up to complex animal behaviors. Coincidentally, a psychology class changed the focus of my career while psychotherapy changed my approach to taking tests.

Physiological Psychology was taught by a wonderful professor, Dr. Owen Floody. Dr. Floody's approach to teaching was so much different than the memory overload we got in biology classes. He took his time to really think about the material, and he expected his students to do the same. Some students thought it was dry and boring, but I was never more into a class in my life. Over the next few years, I took every course Owen Floody taught at Bucknell. My favorite was Human Neuropsychology, which helped me to realize what type of doctor I wanted to be—a neuropsychologist.

The intensity of my positive feelings the day I finally received my Ph.D. came from the realization that all the work, stress, uncertainty, and soul-searching finally paid off. It was a natural high that *I* created. No one in my family had ever heard of neuropsychology, let along knew you could get a doctorate in it.

I've truly come to feel that the pursuit of natural highs is such a personal journey that perhaps the best ones are the ones you create. The remainder of this chapter focuses on the creation of your own natural high. There's a story about pursuing a natural high–based career, ideas from students about activities they do to get naturally high, and a season-by-season outline of natural highs throughout the year. The ultimate goal is to encourage you to take ideas beyond this book and start exploring activities that give you a natural high.

Into the Wild

For thousands of years, human beings lived close to forests and bodies of water to help them obtain food and shelter. Humans today can live just about anywhere on the planet thanks to the food industry, among other entities, which saves us tremendous time and energy. The upside is we have more time to recreate or write books, but the downside is we spend more time in cars and stores getting the things we need. If the natural high you'd like to create involves being outdoors, then you'll need to find a balance between modern life and getting back to nature.

The Jon Krakauer book *Into the Wild* (and 2007 movie by the same name) captured the human instinct to be one with nature. However, it also showed how the obsessive pursuit of being outdoors can be isolating and dangerous. If you feel the strong pull of wanting to live closer to the elements, perhaps you'll consider a career that takes you closer to natural beauty on a daily basis.

One of my oldest friends from high school, Paul Brown, created his own natural high and made a career out of it. Paul's natural high is experiencing wildlife up close. Where we grew up, "wildlife" usually includes things like a parrot on someone's shoulder or the animals that live in people's garbage. Despite this, from an early age Paul exhibited an interest in all things outdoors. I found it interesting to learn that no one in his family fostered this love for the wild—it was his own thing that he just picked up.

Paul attended Ramapo College in New Jersey where he studied environmental science. After graduation, he was volunteering with a hawk watch in New Jersey and working at an outdoor store, but dreamed of heading west. In my opinion, Paul seemed miserable living and working a non-wildlife-related job. The only time he perked up was when we were fishing, or when he talked about traveling to places like Utah, Wyoming, and Colorado.

I recently talked to Paul about his first trip out west. "Seeing snow in the summer and smelling that mountain air blew me away," he said. "I fell in love easily with the wildlife and the sense of wilderness. You realize that when you're not on top of the food chain, you have to use all of your senses—like smell and hearing. I loved it."

Paul first lived in Utah and got a job with the Forest Service, but soon ran out of money and had to return home to plan how he would make a living. On a vacation to Jackson, Wyoming, to visit a friend he discovered the place that would eventually bring him back—Yellowstone National Park. Yellowstone was the nation's first national park and is roughly the size of Delaware and Rhode Island combined. (At least that's what Paul tells me.) His love for Yellowstone was so strong that it finally motivated him to make a change.

"Moving back to New Jersey was a big letdown," he said. "I wasn't happy and I missed the feeling of being around so much wildlife. It was depressing to work at a job just to make money. It was actually dreadful."

What always fascinated me about Paul's story was that despite his depressed feelings, he took a risk and did something about his situation. There are so many people who become paralyzed when they realize that they are miserable in their own life. They do nothing and think things will get better. Paul told me, "If you really want something, you can make it work. It helped that I was young and had the desire to experience different things."

I've visited Paul several times in Jackson, Wyoming. It's great to see what a terrific life he's got going today. I'll admit, it took me a little while to understand Paul's wildlife natural high. It's such a different landscape for me that I was initially out of my comfort zone. The moment I realized that I was really starting to feel the natural high was the sense that I lost track of time. We were out paddling on the Snake River and the vastness of the mountains coupled with the beauty of the river made me feel like minutes had passed when it had been hours.

Paul's favorite natural high involves wolf watching. His entire mood changes when he's talking about those animals. "I get an instant adrenaline rush when I spot wolves," he remarked. "If I'm taking guests out on a tour and we see some wolves, I get very excited because it's fun watching others get psyched. These are rare animals that people traveled thousands of miles to see and I am showing it to them—that is a natural high. If the animals break into a chase, my heart races, I start talking really fast, and I lose all track of time."

Today, Paul works for the Teton Science School in Jackson Hole, Wyoming, giving tours of Yellowstone Natural Park's wolf habitats. In addition, he takes private groups to Hudson Bay in Canada to watch polar bears. These activities may or may not be your thing, but I admire Paul's ability to integrate his favorite natural highs with his career.

Meditating

As an eighth grader, I had two things going for me: I was athletic and tall. Well, OK, I've never been tall, but at five foot eight I was tallish for eighth grade. My problem was that I would only grow one more inch over the next five years of growing. It's not my fault. I'm tall for an Italian. In Italy, I'm like Shaq.

Anyway, in eighth grade I played center on my community league basketball team. (Calling it a team is being generous, because we had like two kids who could shoot.) During one game I scored 70 points and we won 72 to 70. I guess I was a bit of ball hog. The point is that I was an amazing basketball player for one year of my life. It was the year before kids my age grew and the year I learned to meditate.

We had a motivational speaker come to address the league and I remember one thing about his talk. He said that players who visualized themselves making baskets in the game before they went out to play were proven to score more points than those who did not visualize. It turned out to be great advice.

Prior to games, I started crawling into the closet in my room, turning out the lights, and visualizing myself scoring points and winning the game. Our team went from average to competing for the league championship in about a month. I can still recall how peaceful it felt to walk into the arena after my meditation sessions. It was like nothing bothered me. There was almost no anxiety—and no question in my mind that I could win the game.

I certainly would not say that my little basketball meditation experiment is proof that meditation works. First of all, no one showed me what to do or talked me through the visualization. However, I believed so much in visualizing in a dark room that I even used it again later in life.

The first several times I started doing stand-up comedy I used visualization to walk myself through my set. I would visualize the stage, the audience, and me—crushing of course. The first time I tried the exercise, I was doing a gig at the Pizzeria Uno's off of South Street in Philadelphia. There were no dark rooms there, so I made sure to meditate at home. It was a big night. My in-laws were in the crowd and I wanted them to know I was the best comedian to ever work a Pizzeria Uno's.

The gig was actually a lot of fun. The audience was happy,

which can save even the worst comedian. More importantly, I think I did well because I slowed down my pace. In my previous sets, I would speak so fast that I was stepping on the laughs. But the Uno's gig was different. I was so calm and focused that I was really able to be in the moment and make my act feel very natural.

Feeling calm and centered is a state of natural high. Many people use drugs to attain a sense of calm, but you can achieve this state in a healthier way. You may not even realize that with training in meditation you can improve your ability to sit peacefully. It sounds like it would be the easiest thing in the world, but it's not. It requires practice to sit with your eyes closed and think about nothing. My visualization exercise was easy compared to trying to think about nothing for more than a few minutes.

Try This: If you feel you've got a stressful event or week coming up, try spending a few minutes a day in a dark room preparing. You could choose to visualize yourself being successful and happy at the end of the week or you could choose to just try and think about nothing. Either way, this activity will likely change how you feel about the upcoming event. When it's over, make note of any physical or emotional changes you felt during the stressful period. Do you feel better physically or have a sense of calm? If you enjoy how you're feeling, you may want to learn more about meditation at www.tmeducation.org.

Pick Your Brain:
Meditating

There are many documented benefits of meditation, including improved immune functioning, deeper sleep, reduced levels of anxiety, and improved mood.[1,2,3] In recent years, meditative practices have been implemented in hospitals and academic medical centers to help soothe patients with chronic stress and pain-related disorders.

Neuroscientists have also become interested in the relationship between meditation, brain activity, and immune system functioning.

For example: stressful life events have been shown to negatively impact the benefits of receiving a flu shot.[4] Researchers studied this phenomenon by measuring the amount of antibodies produced following the flu shot in older adults experiencing chronic stress. However, you could imagine a similar study with young people living with poverty, domestic violence, or regularly dealing with a bully. Normally, when someone receives the flu vaccine, their antibody levels increase. However, caregivers showed a poorer antibody response following vaccination, compared with a control group of non-chronically stressed people.

Based on this result, researchers at the Laboratory of Affective Neuroscience at the University of Wisconsin hypothesized that meditation might have the opposite effect on immune functioning.[1] To test their idea, they measured antibody titers in individuals who underwent an eight-week trial of meditation. They also measured brain electrical activity before, immediately after, and four months following the meditation training.

The researchers found significant increases in flu vaccine antibody titers after receiving the shot in those who received the meditation training, as compared with a control group. In addition, measures of brain electrical activity showed increased activity in the anterior left hemisphere, an area shown in previous studies to be associated with positive affect[5]—that is, feeling good.

Meditating appears to be more about calm, focus, and positive feelings than euphoria. For those willing to pursue meditation, you may want to do it following that annual flu shot—your immune system could even receive more benefit from the shot than it would normally. The only downside to meditating seems to be trying to find someplace quiet in which to do it. I can tell you from personal experience that closets are not the best-smelling places in the world.

Paintball, Dude

In creating your own natural high, it helps if you're willing to try new things. This sometimes involves taking social risks, too. As I discussed in the first chapter, my inspiration for creating the student group C.A.L.V.I.N. & H.O.B.B.E.S. was that I was not happy as a Bucknell student. I was faced with a choice: I could either change my school and leave, or change the school and do something about it.

One of my favorite C&H events was paintball. Central Pennsylvania has one of the best paintball facilities in the country: Skirmish USA. They have dozens of paintball fields with names like "Amazon Jungle" and "Z-Swamp." I can't remember which of our C&H members suggested the event, but when you have a group of 40-plus young people, you have the makings for a great event.

The only problem was money. It was going to cost about $30 per person, plus another $20 for paint, transportation, and lunch for the day. Multiply that by 40 students and you have an event that was going to cost $2,000. We only had $1,000.

Then we had a brilliant idea which would not only enable us all to go but would also generate a lot of great buzz about C&H. We set aside enough money for 20 spots, then held a campus raffle for the other 20 spots: one dollar per ticket and the winners play for free. It was a huge success! The raffle generated an additional $1,000 because students were happy to risk a few dollars for an outing that could easily cost $50.

The day of the event was one of those perfect fall days. We drove out to Skirmish USA in vans and I watched as students sat quietly in their little cliques. Once we arrived, we split everyone up into two teams of 20. It turned out that we brought a big enough group to be assigned to our own field with our own officials.

We spent the day battling around trees, crawling through streams, and generally running around like maniacs. At one point, I remember getting hit in that one spot that isn't protected. No, not that one. I mean my neck. When those paintballs hit my skin and burst, I looked down in panic and yelled, "Is it blood? Oh no, is it blood?" To which someone next to me said, "It's green."

The ride home from the event said it all. In the vans, there were no more barriers between people, just friends telling "war" stories. Everyone had bonded over a shared experience. We were all exhausted because we had gone through so many emotions on the field—fear, surprise, euphoria. It was great seeing that so many students were genuinely thankful that we'd put on the event. It was almost as if they didn't believe they could have that much fun in college.

Try This: Dude, you've got to play paintball! If you're anywhere near eastern Pennsylvania, check out Skirmish USA at www.skirmish.com. If not, there's bound to be a paintball field somewhere near you.

Student Natural Highs List

I recently spoke at several district student council conferences in New Mexico. One of the conferences was in Roswell, New Mexico. Before I left, friends told me jokingly, "You know what's in Roswell? They have aliens there." The four-hour drive from Albuquerque—in the dark—was so mind-numbingly straight that I could have fallen asleep and still arrived safely.

I was about an hour outside of Roswell when it happened. I saw several lights dancing in the sky in a coordinated pattern. They darted in toward the middle and then out. I thought, "My friends were right! The aliens are here."

It turned out to be a Walmart grand opening in the distance. Undies were half off that week.

During the conferences, I presented a workshop that involved students creating a list of natural high activities that they considered as much fun as going to a traditional party with alcohol, etc. The events they came up with were creative, simple, and inexpensive. Here is the complied list from all of the groups

- Movie under the stars
- Scavenger hunt
- Sports tournament
- Giant Slip 'n Slide party
- Murder mystery party
- Open mike / coffeehouse
- Mud volleyball tournament
- Battle of the bands
- Rock-n-bowl
- Video game tournament
- Camping trip
- Karaoke party

• Lock-in event (an overnight party where students can't enter after a certain hour); the activities can include many of the above

I'm often asked for ideas on what events students' groups can organize, but I think it's best for each individual group to define what their event will look like. If you have a small group, then suggesting that the National Guard come and dig trenches for your mud volleyball event is probably unrealistic. If you have over 500 students then a camping trip wouldn't be something that is logistically feasible. So, I suggest that each unique group apply their own local flavor to make any event special.

It seemed like quite a coincidence that, soon after compiling this list, I saw a television commercial for hard liquor that included people drinking at a giant Slip 'n Slide party. If you see the ad, you'll notice that there is virtually nothing in the ad about alcohol, except that they paired it with a great Slip 'n Slide event.

I find it flattering that alcohol companies are turning to natural highs to sell their products, but do they really need to spoil the true spirit of a *natural* high? This phenomenon is not a new one. When I was younger, they tried to convince us that alcohol would bring more loving natural highs involving young men and women in bikinis. And when I was in my twenties, the commercials seemed to be all about the laughter natural high, as the commercials took a decidedly funny turn. I don't expect the runner's high to be paired with alcohol anytime soon. That could get ugly.

Try This: If you have a group that's looking to put on a social event, try one of the events suggested by the New Mexico students. They can be tailored for groups of all ages. The older folks may need some supervision, but everyone else should be fine.

Outrunning Negativity

If you're going to attempt new things in life, like paintball, meditating, or eating new foods, you might face some resistance. Some of it may be well intended, like those who want you to avoid hypothermia when you're surfing Lake Erie in January. However, others will simply be projecting their own negative thoughts about the activity onto you by saying, "You can't do that!" or "What's wrong with you?"

Unfortunately, this type of dismissive feedback from others can often put an end to a lot of positive risk-taking behaviors by putting people on the defensive.

I suggest two approaches to dealing with negative people when ignoring them is not an option. First, it will likely be helpful to let the person know how they make you feel. Doing so might make them more aware of what they're saying. When I was in college, I would often use the line "Are you trying to be a jerk or are you just getting lucky?" Of course, you might find it more productive to say something like "I don't really find your comments supportive. What would make you say something like that?" If the other person doesn't seem to care that they've hurt your feelings, you may want to consider that the next time you think about sharing something with them.

A second approach to dealing with the chronically negative is to try to empathize with them. Yes, that's right—caring more about their feelings than they care about yours. Empathy, or putting yourself in someone else's shoes, can actually give you insight into what motivates their negativity. The person may have grown up in an abusive environment where negativity was the norm. They may be feeling miserable about their own current life situation, thereby making it difficult for them to be happy for you. They could also just be a jerk, but that explanation is far less interesting.

Research shows that people who are constantly negative in the words they use and the reactions they have are probably not the most mentally healthy people.[6] Remember—you have a choice when it comes to who you lean on for emotional support. Finding people who love you and who'll be there for you is important, but also look for people who themselves are happy individuals. People who have the ability to be genuinely happy for you are often those who can really listen to you when you have a problem.

Try This: Make a list of the five most positive people and the five most negative people in your life. Then assign each person with a number from 0 to 5, 0 being the least positive/negative and 5 being the most positive/negative. When you're finished, examine each entry and write down why you gave each person the rating that you did. You may decide that, after creating your list, you have very few negative influences in your life.

But if this is not the case, you may want to think about some coping strategies for dealing with the negative individuals. I've found that often, the people in life who affect us most negatively can be those we're forced to deal with on a daily basis. The easy solution would be to distance yourself from these people, especially when you're stressed or feeling down. If you cannot distance yourself from the negative influences, then consider expressing your feelings to the person or to someone who listens well. The process of putting your feelings into words can help you feel better or at least invite another perspective on the situation. If all else fails, remember to turn to your natural highs. They are your healthiest coping skills, especially when a situation is not changing anytime soon. Go out for a run, learn how to paint, laugh with a friend, or help someone in need. These activities will make you feel better and provide a healthy distraction from day-to-day stress.

By the way, I did this positive/negative exercise in ninth grade and found it gave me tremendous insight into my friends and family. Give it a try.

My Best Natural High Day

My birthday is in December. Just once, it would be cool to have a birthday during a warm-weather month or at least far away from a month during which everyone spends all of their money. When I was in my twenties, I used to think about the perfect day for my birthday and try to make it happen. I would do a few things that I love doing in December, like sleeping late, reading, and keeping my body temperature normal. And then I'd visit my favorite restaurant at night. Over the years, I've expanded this concept of the "best day." I've added ideas from friends, family, and my audience members to come up with the best natural high day for each season. I've tried to make my list include experiences and items of all price ranges, from "free" to "great if money was no object." I'll admit the list is biased toward places that I've visited—they're just too great to leave out. Hopefully my list will encourage you to consider *your* list.

Best Day: Summer

Location: Anywhere near the water—lake or ocean

My Favorite Spot: Ocean City, New Jersey (great waves, tons of stuff to do)

1. Wake up late and get in the water (with a friend or someone watching, of course). There are few things that will change how you feel faster than jumping into water first thing in the morning.
2. Make yourself some killer brunch food like chocolate chip pancakes or a California omelet with avocado and tomatoes.
3. Go to the gym, ride a bike, or take a nap.
4. In the afternoon, get to the beach with friends and, of course, spend more time in the water. Try a new water sport, like skim-boarding, bodysurfing, or tubing.
5. Read, throw a football, sit on the beach, or just stare at the water.
6. Have a summer romance.
7. End the day by grabbing a sweatshirt, sitting on the sand, and watching the sunset. At the lake, it's amazing watching the fish feeding off the hatching bugs and at the ocean, it's great to watch the water calm down.
8. Eat on the beach or get out on the town for a great meal. No matter where you are, in my opinion fresh summer tomatoes should be involved.
9. After dinner, go out people-watching. Walking the boardwalk or around town is a great way to enjoy the parade of all kinds of folks having fun.
10. Ice cream! My personal recommendations: Kohr's Custard (Ocean City, New Jersey), Ben & Jerry's (Cape Cod, Massachusetts), or if you're landlocked, Ted Drewes (St. Louis, Missouri) and Graeters (Cincinnati, Ohio).

Best Day: Fall

Location: Anywhere in America, but the highlights are the East Coast for the leaves, West Coast for the weather

My Favorite Spot: New York City

1. Go to a farmer's market and buy a pumpkin. Try leaf peeping, a hayride, or watch the local high school or college football game.
2. Have a picnic outside as the leaves begin to fall.

3. Help a neighbor or someone less fortunate than you, especially around the holidays.
4. Enter a road race, get in some late-season golf, or take a long bike ride and go exploring. My personal recommendation: play paintball with friends.
5. Enjoy a nice post-workout lunch. My personal recommendation: egg and cheese on a bagel. Delish!
6. Stay up late watching the baseball playoffs on television or an NFL game.

Best Day: Winter

Location: In the mountains, preferably with snow

My Favorite Spot: The Berkshire Mountains in Massachusetts

1. If you're staying with friends or family, wake up and help your hosts by doing some chores, like chopping wood or shoveling show.
2. Eat a warm breakfast with some hot chocolate or anything that feels cozy. My personal recommendation: a chai tea latte with cinnamon.
3. Get on the snow gear and go out for a day of snowboarding, skiing, tubing, snowmobiling, cross-country skiing, snowshoeing, or just have a great game of football in the snow.
4. Return from the great outdoors, eat a hearty meal, and warm up reading a book, playing a board game with friends, or watching a movie. My personal recommendation: *The Shawshank Redemption.*
5. Make a fire in a fireplace or huddle with friends for warmth.
6. Take a nap—winter is made for napping.
7. Spend extra time hanging out with friends.

Best Day: Spring

Location: Anywhere it starts to warm up first

My Favorite Spot: Hilton Head Island, South Carolina

1. Go for a run or a bike ride to take in the sights, smells, and sounds of spring.
2. Volunteer your time—spring is a time of renewal and increased energy.
3. Plant a tree or flowers, or create a vegetable garden.
4. Play softball in the park with friends or get tickets to an early season baseball game.

5. Make dinner for someone—it's always better to give than to receive! My personal recommendation: ribollita (you heard me raving about it in Chapter 4).

6. Fall asleep thinking about the great upcoming summer adventures.

Try This: Describe, in writing, your "Best Natural High Day" for each season of the year. If you cannot come up with enough experiences that you know give you a consistent natural high in each season, then get to work finding them! Some people say, "I hate the winter [or summer, or whatever] around here." However, if they had natural highs in place for each season, they might find within themselves the ability to love life a little more.

Wrap-Up

The best natural highs are the ones that you create to fit your life, and your life plan. The everyday ones—like running, hanging out with good friends and sharing a meal, helping someone in need—are more easily achieved. Others, more ambitious or requiring longer commitments, are often referred to as dreams or goals, but when you do achieve them, the feelings they impart are truly natural highs. If your natural high involves academic achievement, moving to an exotic land, or attaining some inner peace, it may take time. The natural high you ultimately experience is something unique to you. You really are the only one who can determine how it feels or if it's worth pursuing. In the end, the time you spend finding your natural high will always feel worth it.

Regardless of the natural high you choose, there might be obstacles to achieving that high. Lack of time or money, for example, or being around negative people will often be reminders that pursuing something that's great for you might not always be easy. However, when you're doing something positive for yourself, it is always worth the effort. Remembering that will help to keep you going. If you need a little reminder and you don't have 20 minutes to read the book again (I know, it just feels quick), check this shortcut of natural highs and the effects. It's almost like the text message version of my book!

Good luck pursuing your natural highs! I would love to hear about them if you get a chance. Just shoot me an e-mail with your story at matt@mattbellace.com.

Natural High (NH)	How to Achieve the NH	Feelings Associated with the NH	Neurochemical(s) Associated with the NH	Drugs Used to Achieve Similar Feelings
Laughing	Hanging out with friends; watching funny movies, stand-up comedy	Euphoria; happiness; sense of well-being	Dopamine; norepinephrine; serotonin	Alcohol, in small amounts (happiness); cocaine and amphetamines (euphoria); ecstasy (sense of well-being)
Running	Distance running; surfing; biking; skiing; any activity that significantly elevates heart rate	Euphoria; calm; focused; reduced pain sensation; sense of power	Opiates; endorphins; acetylcholine	Marijuana, heroin, and oxycodone (reduced pain, calm, focused); cocaine, alcohol, and amphetamines (euphoria, sense of power)
Eating	Cooking "slow food" at home or eating at a good restaurant – preferably with loved ones	Calm; happiness; reduced hunger pains	Dopamine; serotonin	Nicotine and marijuana (calm); alcohol (happy feelings)
Helping	Volunteering your time to those in need; donating money to good causes	Happiness; sense of connection to others	Oxytocin; dopamine	Alcohol (happy feelings); ecstasy (sense of connection)
Loving	Spending time with family, friends, or romantic partners; becoming immersed in an activity you're passionate about	Euphoria; warm feelings; happiness; sense of connection to others; sense of well-being	Oxytocin; dopamine: norepinephrine; serotonin	Ecstasy (sense of connection, love); alcohol (happy feelings); cocaine and heroin (euphoria and feelings of warmth)
Creating Your Own	Varies (for example, meditating; creating art; outdoor activities)	Varies (for example, meditating produces a sense of calm; being at peace with the world)	Varies (for example, meditating increases serotonin levels)	Varies (for example, acid, psilocybin-containing muchrooms, and marijuana (sense of calm)

Endnotes

Chapter 1: How to Get High Naturally

1. Denizet-Lewis, B. (2006, June 25) An Anti-Addiction Pill. *The New York Times*.

2. Alexander, B., Beyerstein, B., Hadaway, P., & Coambs, R. (1981). Effect of early and later colony housing on oral ingestion of morphine in rats. *Pharmacology Biochemistry and Behavior, 15* (4), 571-576.

3. Gordon, H. (2002). Early environmental stress and biological vulnerability to drug abuse. *Psychoneuroendocrinology, 27,* 115-126.

4. Ompad, D., Ikeda, R., Shah, N., Fuller, C., Bailey, S., Morse, E., Kerndt, P., Maslow, C., Wu, Y., Vlahov, D., Garfein, R., & Strathdee, S. (2005). Childhood sexual abuse and age at initiation of injection drug use. *American Journal of Public Health, 95*(4), 703-709.

5. Pennebaker, J. (1997). Writing about emotional experiences as a therapeutic process. *Psychological Science, 8,* 162-166.

6. Gortner, E., Rude, S., & Pennebaker, J. (2006). Benefits of expressive writing in lowering rumination and depressive symptoms. *Behavior Therapy, 37:* 292-303.

7. Klein, K. (2002). Stress, expressive writing, and working memory. In: S.J. Lepore, & J.M. Smyth (Eds.), *The Writing Cure: How Expressive Writing Promotes Health and Emotional Well-Being* (pp. 135-155). Washington DC: American Psychological Association.

8. Kirk, U., Downer, J., & Montague, R. (2011). Introception Drives Increased Rational Decision-Making in Mediators Playing the Ultimatum Game. *Frontiers in Neuroscience, 5:*49

9. Mobbs, D., Greicius, M., Abdel-Azim, E., Menon, V., & Reiss, A. (2003). Humor modulates the mesolimbic reward centers. *Neuron, 40,*1041-1048.

10. Levy, B., & Earleywine, M. (2004). Discriminating reinforcement expectancies for studying from future time perspective in the prediction of drinking problems. *Addicitve Behaviors, 29,* 181-190.

11. Turrisi, R. (1999). Cognitive and attitudinal factors in the analysis of alternatives to binge drinking. *Journal of Applied Social Psychology, 27*(7), 1512-1535.

12. Correia, C., Benson, T., & Carey, K. (2005). Decreased substance use following increases in alternative behaviors: A preliminary investigation. *Addictive Behaviors, 30*(1), 19-27.

13. Murphy, J., Barnett, N., & Colby, S. (2006). Alcohol-related and alcohol-free activity participation and enjoyment among college students: A behavioral theories of choice analysis. *Experimental and Clinical Psychopharmacology, 14*(3), 339-349.

14. DeJong, W., & Langford, L. (2002). A typology for campus-based alcohol prevention: Moving toward environmental strategies. *Journal of Studies on Alcohol, 14* (Suppl.), 140-147.

15. Geir, T. (1996, January 8). Outlook: Eye on the 90's. *US News and World Report*.

16. Hubel, D., & Wiesel, T. (1977). Ferrier lecture: Functional architecture of macaque monkey visual cortex. *Proceedings of the Royal Society of London- B, 198,* 1-59.

17. Hubel, D., Weisel, T., & LeVay, S. (1977). Plasticity of ocular dominance columns in monkey striate cortex. *Philosophical Transactions of the Royal Society London- B: Biological Sciences, 278,* 377-409.

18. Candland, D. (1993). Feral children and clever animals. Oxford University Press.

19. Harlow, H. & Griffin, G. (1965). Induced mental and social deficits in rhesus monkeys. In S.F. Osler and R.E. Cooke (Eds.), *The Biosocial Basis of Mental Retardation*. Baltimore: Johns Hopkins Press.

20. Giedd, J. (2004). Structural magnetic resonance imaging of the adolescent brain. *Annals of the New York Academy of Sciences, 1021,* 77-85.

Chapter 2: Laughing, Smiling and Other Highs Better Than Cocaine

1. Mobbs, D., Greicius, M., Azim, E., Menon, V., & Reiss, A. (2003). Humor modulates the mesolimbic reward regions. *Neuron. 40*, 1041-1048.
2. Drevets, W., Gautier, C., Price, J., Kupfer, D., Kinahan, P., Grace, A., Price, J., & Mathias, C. (2001). Amphetamine-induced dopamine release in human ventral striatum correlates with euphoria. *Biological Psychiatry, 49*, 81-96.
3. Fry, W. (1994). The biology of humor. *Humor: International Journal of Humor Research, 7*, 111-126.
4. Hayashi, T., Tsujii, S., Iburi, T., Tamanaha, T., Yamagami, K., Ishibashi, R., Hori, M., Sakamoto, S., Ishii, H., & Murakami, K. (2007). Laughter up-regulates the gene related to NK cell activity in diabetes. 2007. *Biomedical Research. 28*(6), 281-285.
5. Research Report Series, Cocaine: Abuse and Addiction. Retrieved November 23, 2011 from http://www.nida.nih.gov/researchreports/cocaine/effects.html

Chapter 3: Running, Surfing and Other Highs Better Than Weed

1. Boecker, H., Sprenger, T., Henriksen, G., Koppenhoefer, M., Wagner, K., Valet, M., Berthele, A., & Tolle, T. (2008). The Runner's High: Opioidergic mechanisms in the human brain. *Cerebral Cortex*. Advanced Access published February 21, 2008.
2. Brown, R., Abrantes, A., Read, J., Marcus, B., Jakicic, J., Strong, D., Oakley, J., Ramsey, S., Kahler, C., Stuart, G., Dubreil, M., & Gordon, A. (2009). Aerobic exercise for alcohol recovery: Rationale, program description and preliminary findings. *Behavior Modification. 33*(2), 220-249.
3. Scott, P. (2006). Fitness: Bodies in motion clean and sober. *The New York Times*. October 12, 2006.
4. Sparling, P., Giuffrida, A., Piomelli, D., Rosskopf, L. & Dietrich, A. (2003). Exercise activates the endocannabinoid system. *Cognitive Neuroscience and Neuropsychology, 14* (17), 2209-2211.
5. Yucel, M., Solowij, N., Respondek, C., Whittle, S., Fornito, A., Pantelis, C. & Lubman, D. (2008). Regional brain abnormalities associated with long-term heavy cannabis use. *Archives of General Psychiatry, 65* (6), 694-701.
6. Chaddock, L., Erickson, K., Prakash, R., Kim, J., Voss, M., VanPatter, M., Pontifex, M., Raine, L., Konkel, A., Hillman, C., Cohen, N, & Kramer, A. (2010). A neuroimaging investigation of the association between aerobic fitness, hippocampal volume, and memory performance in preadolescent children. *Brain Research, 1358*, 172-183.
7. Volkow, N., Wang, G, & Tomasi, D. (2014). Decreased dopamine brain reactivity in marijuana abusers is associated with negative emotionality and addiction severity. *Proceedings of the National Academy of Science USA, 111*(30), E3149-E3156.
8. Baum, S., Ma., J., Payae, K., (2013). Education Pays 2013. Retrieved September 9, 2014, from http://trends.collegeboard.org/sites/default/files/education-pays-2013-full-report.pdf
9. Fergusson, D. & Boden, J. (2008). Cannabis use and later life outcomes. *Addiction, 103* (6):969-976.
10. Silins, E., Horwood, J., Patton, G., Fergusson, D., Olsson, C., Hutchinson, D., Spry, E., Toumbourou, J., Degenhardt, L., Swift, W., Coffey, C., Tait, R., Letcher, P., Copeland, J. & Mattick, R. (2014). Young adult sequelae of adolescent cannabis use: an integrative analysis. *The Lancet Psychiatry, 1*(4): 286-293.
11. Meier, M, Caspi, A., Ambler, A., Harrington, H., Houts, R., Keefe, R., McDonald, K., Ward, A., Pouton, R. & Moffit, T. (2012). Persistent cannabis users show neuropsychological declines from childhood to midlife. *Proceedings of National Academy of Sciences, 109* (40), E2657-E2664.
12. Lynskey, M., Glowinski, A., Todorov, A., Bucholz, K., Madden, P., Nelson, E., Statham, D., Martin, N., & Heath, A. (2004). Major depressive disorder, suicidal

ideation, suicide attempt, in twins discordant for cannabis dependence and early-onset cannabis use. *Archives of General Psychiatry*, 61:1026-1032.

13. Large, M., Sharma, S., Compton, M., Slade, T., Nielssen, O. (2011). Cannabis use and earlier onset of psychosis. *Archives of General Psychiatry*, 68(6):555-61.

14. Terman, M., Terman, J. & Ross, D. (1998). A controlled trial of timed bright light and negative air ionization for treatment of winter depression. *Archives of General Psychiatry*, *55*, 875-882.

15. Goel, N. & Etwaroo, G. (2006). Bright light, negative air ions and auditory stimuli produce rapid mood changes in a student population: A placebo-controlled study. *Psychological Medicine, 36*, 1253-1263.

Chapter 4: Eating, Cooking and Other Highs Better Than Alcohol

1. Davis, C., Levitan, R., Reid, C., Carter, J., Kaplan, A., Patte, K., King, N., & Kennedy, J. (2009). Dopamine for "wanting" and opioids for "liking": A comparison of obese adults with and without binge eating. *Obesity,* March, 12: E-publication ahead of print, p. 1-6.

2. Hayward, M., & Low, M. (2005). Naloxone's suppression of spontaneous and food-conditioned locomotor activity is diminished in mice lacking either the dopamine D(s) receptor or enkephalin. *Brain Research: Molecular Brain Research, 140*, 91-98.

3. Avena, N., Rada, P., & Hoebel, B. (2009). Sugar and fat bingeing have notable differences in addictive-like behavior. *The Journal of Nutrition, 139*, 623-628.

4. Avena, N., Bocarsly, M., Rada, P., Kim, A. & Hoebel, B. (2008). After daily bingeing on a sucrose solution, food deprivation induces anxiety and accumbens dopamine/acetylcholine imbalance. *Physiology & Behavior, 94*, 309-315.

5. Allen, N., Beral, V., Casabonne, D., Kan, S., Reeves, G., Brown, A., & Green, J. (2009). Moderate alcohol intake and cancer incidence in woman. *Journal of the National Cancer Institute, 101* (5), 296-305.

6. Paul, C., Au, R., Fredman, L., Massaro, J., Seshadri, S., DeCarli, C. & Wolf, P. (2008). Association of alcohol consumption with brain volume in the Framingham study. *Archives of Neurology, 65* (10), 1363-1367.

Chapter 5: Helping, Listening and Other Highs Better Than Being Selfish

1. Giving USA (2006). *The Annual Report on Philanthropy for the Year 2006*. Giving Institute.

2. Moll, J., Krueger, F., Zahn, R., Pardini, M., Olivera-Souza, R., & Grafman, J. (2006). Human fronto-mesolimbic networks guide decisions about charitable donation. *Proceedings of the National Academy of Sciences, 103* (42), 15623-15628.

3. Zak, P., Stanton, A., & Ahmadi, S. (2007). Oxytocin increases generosity in humans. *Public Library of Science, One, 2*(11): e1128.

4. Tankersley, D., Stowe C., & Huettel S. (2007). Altruism is associated with an increased neural response to agency. *Nature Neuroscience, 10*(2), 150-151.

Chapter 6: Loving, Caring and Other Highs Better Than Hurting Yourself

1. Zeki, S. (2007). The neurobiology of love. *Federation of European Biological Societies. 581*, 2575-2579.

2. O'Connor, M., Wellisch, D., Stanton, A., Eisenberger, N., Irwin, M., & Lieberman, M. (2008). Craving love? Enduring grief activates brain's reward center. *NeuroImage 42* (2), 969-972.

3. Insel, T. (2003). Is social attachment an addictive disorder? *Physiology and Behavior, 79* (3), 351.

Chapter 7: Unhealthy Natural Highs

1. Welte, J, Barnes, G, Tidwell, M, & Hoffman, J. (2008). The prevalence of problem gambling among U.S. adolescents and young adults: Results from a national survey. *Journal of Gambling Studies, 24,* 119-133.

2. Toneatto, T. & Dragonetti, R. (2008). Effectiveness of community-based treatment for problem gambling: A quasi-experimental evaluation of cognitive-behavioral vs. twelve-step therapy. *The American Journal on Addictions, 17,* 298-303.

3. Dodd, M, Klos, K, Bower, J, Geda, Y, Josephs, K, & Ahlskog, E. (2005). Pathological gambling caused by drugs used to treat Parkinson's Disease. *Archives of Neurology, Vol 62,* 1377-1388.

4. Volkow, N, Wang, G, Fowler, & Telang, F. (2008). Overlapping neuronal circuits in addiction and obesity: Evidence of systems pathology. *Philosophical Transactions of the Royal Society of London. Series B, Biological Sciences, 363* (1507), 3191-3200.

5. Torgan, C. (2002). Childhood obesity on the rise. Retrieved October 3, 2009, from http://www.nih.gov/news/WordonHealth/jun2002/childhoodobesity.htm

6. Trasande, L. & Chatterjee, S. (2009). The impact of obesity on health service utilization and costs in childhood. *Obesity,* March 19.

7. Sacks, F, Bray, G, Carey, V, Smith, S, & Ryan, D (2009). Comparison of weight-loss diets with different compositions of fat, protein, and carbohydrates. *The New England Journal of Medicine, 360,* 859-873.

8. Mond, J, Hay, P, Rodgers, B, & Owen, C. (2006) An update on the definition of "excessive exercise" in eating disorder research. *International Journal of Eating Disorders, 39,* 147-153.

9. Fuss, J., Ben Abdallah, N., Vogt, M., Touma, C., Pacifici, P., Palme, R., Witzemann, V., Hellweg, R. & Gass, P. (2010). Voluntary exercise induces anxiety-like behavior in adult c57bl/6j mice correlating with hippocampal neurogenesis. *Hippocampus, 20,* 364-376.

10. Shroff, H, Reba, L, Thornton, L, Tozzi, F, Klump, K, et al. (2006). Features associated with excessive exercise in women with eating disorders. *International Journal of Eating Disorders. 39* (6), 454-461.

11. Field, A, Cheung, L, Wolf, A, Herzog, D, Gortmaker, S, & Colditz, G. (1999). Exposure to the mass media and weight concern among girls. *Pediatrics, 103,* E53.

12. Caine, D., & Watson, J., (2000). Neuropsychological effects of anoxic or ischemic induced brain injury. *Journal of the International Neuropsychological Society, 10,* 957-961.

13. Hopkins, R. & Haaland, K. (2004). Neuropsychological effects of anoxic or ischemic induced brain injury. *Journal of the International Neuropsychological Society, 10,* 957-961.

14. Brown, L, Houck, C, Grossman, C, Lescano, C, & Frenkel, J. (2008). Frequency of adolescent self-cutting as a predictor of HIV risk. *Journal of Developmental and Behavioral Pediatrics, Vol 29* (3), 161-165.

15. Suyemoto, K. (1998). The functions of self-mutilation. *Clinical Psychology Review, 18* (5), 531-554.

Chapter 8: Creating—Your Own Natural High

1. Davidson, R., Kabat-Zinn, J., Schumacher, J., Rosenkranz, M., Muller, D., Santorelli, S., Urbanowski, F., Harrington, A., Bonus, K., & Sheridan, J. (2003). Alterations in brain and immune function produced by mindfulness meditation. *Psychosomatic Medicine, 65,* 564-570.

2. Patra, S & Telles, S. (2009). Positive impact of cyclic meditation on subsequent sleep. *Medical Science Monitor, 15*(7), 375-381.

3. Teasdale, J, Williams, J, Soulsby, J, Segal, Z, Ridgeway, V & Lau, M. (2000). Prevention of relapse/recurrence in major depression by mindfulness-based cognitive therapy. *Journal of Consulting and Clinical Psychology, 68*(4), 615-623.

4. Kiecolt-Glaser, J., Glaser, R., Gravenstein, S., Malarkey, W., Sheridan, J. (1996). Chronic stress alters the immune response to influenza virus vaccine in older adults. *Proceedings of the National Academy of Science, USA, 93*, 3043-3047.

5. Davidson, R. (1992). Emotion and affective style: Hemispheric substrates. *Psychological Science, 3*, 39-43.

6. Mathews, A. & MacLeod, C. (2005). Cognitive vulnerability to emotional disorders, *Annual Review of Clinical Psychology, 1*:167-195.

CPSIA information can be obtained
at www.ICGtesting.com
Printed in the USA
BVHW030500150119
537590BV00004BB/9/P

9 781936 214563